design it, knit it

Debbie Bliss

secrets from the designer's studio

design it, knit it

knit it
Debbie Bliss

secrets
from the
designer's
studio

sixth&spring
books

sixth&spring books

233 Spring Street New York, New York 10013

Editors: Michelle Bredeson, Erin Slonaker, Wendy Williams

Technical Editor: Rosy Tucker

Art Director: Diane Lamphron

Associate Art Director: Sheena T. Paul

Copy Editor: Kristina Sigler

Technical Illustrations: Jane Fay

Creative Director: Joe Vior

Production Manager: David Joinnides

Vice President, Publisher: Trisha Malcolm

President: Art Joinnides

Library of Congress Control Number: 2008936331

ISBN-10: 1-933027-76-2

ISBN-13: 978-1-933027-76-0

Manufactured in China

3 5 7 9 10 8 6 4 2

First Edition

contents

design it, knit it

I have always had a passion for design. As a young child I was happy cutting up remnants of fabric, draping them around my dolls or teddies until I got the look I wanted, and then sewing them up with a haphazard backstitch. I still remember the feeling of pride at finishing a rather inappropriately tight tweed pencil skirt with a frilled hem for my beloved baby doll. Yet years later while studying fashion and textiles at art college, I sometimes found myself struggling to create the shapes and styles I'd envisioned—especially when the fabrics didn't always have the life or drape that I'd hoped for. Wandering into a studio one day, where students were working away on a knitting machine, I realized that the knit fabric had everything I was looking for. Ultimately this revelation led to me rediscover hand knitting, which gave me both the textures and shapes that I wanted.

As a designer now for over twenty-five years, I still feel the same excitement I felt then in trying to achieve the prettiest Fair Isle or putting together a sequence of cables to find the most perfect match, while also thinking about how the fabric will behave on the body and how to create the shape I want.

In *Design It, Knit It,* I would like to share with you the creative and practical journey I take when I design a hand knit. It is not a technical book as such, but rather a way to convey my enthusiasm and love for the craft and give you some insights that will set you on the path to creating your own designs.

Debbie Bliss

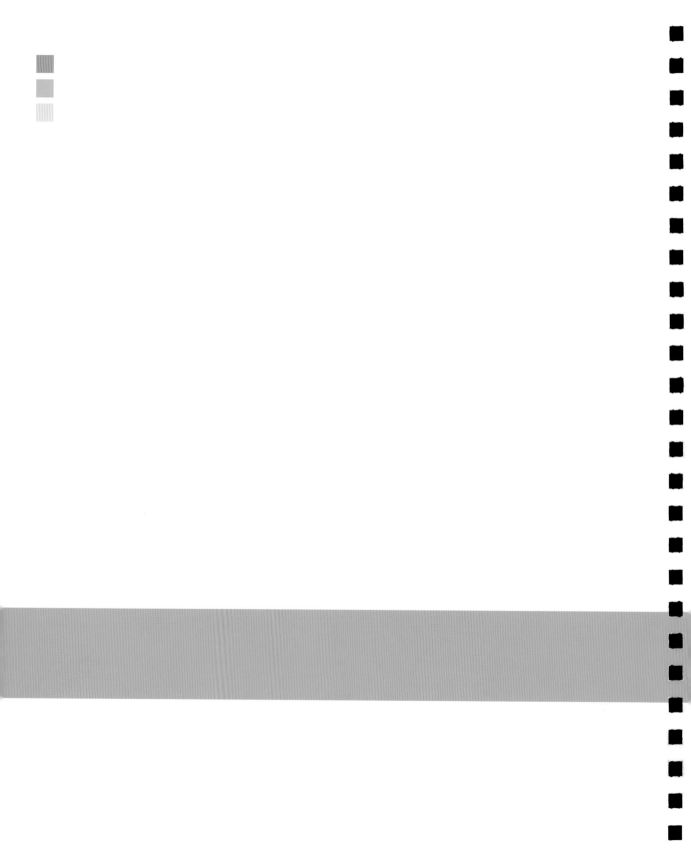

1 designing for the body

designing for the body

I have been very lucky in that in the last twenty years my career has covered both designing fashion knitwear and children's wear. Until I had my own children, my work had been pretty much exclusively designing for adults, mostly women. I find both types of design immensely rewarding in different ways—I love working with babies and toddlers, right from the initial concepts to the chaos and fun of the photo shoots. While on the fashion shoots I love seeing the collection coming together and working with the dedicated team of photographers, stylists and models. It is usually at this point that the knits really come alive for me.

Even before I began designing, I collected vintage patterns, particularly from the 1930s and '40s, and I loved that there was so much attention given to detail in the shaping. At the beginning of my career, the fashion was very much for generous sweaters in T shapes—basically two squares for the body and two rectangles for the sleeves, knitted on large needles in chunky yarns. Starting with these shapes when I was commissioned to design knits for magazines was a great way to learn to create patterns, with the guidance of some very supportive knitting editors. Still, the styles I knitted for myself were from my vintage pattern collection, and this was a wonderful way to discover how the knitted fabric could be sculpted into body-forming shapes. Styles were tailored, shaped into the body at the waist and out again, or widened up from the ribs to the armholes. There were different styles of sleeve heads, from long and narrow to create a pretty puffed sleeve to short and wide to form a square, Joan Crawford style. I enjoyed knitting in the very fine yarns, too, which made an interesting contrast to the heavier-weight yarns I was using for my commissioned designs. Working up these old patterns gave me a grounding in how to shape and tailor in the knitted fabric.

In the same way that the designers who created those patterns wanted to produce modern styles, I need to be aware of fashion trends when I am creating a collection, because most of us want to dress in a stylish, contemporary way. Having been involved in knitwear for many years, I am only too aware that it can be seen as the poor sister of the fashion world; even now people can be rather dismissive not only of the craft but of its place within the design world. I am delighted that in the last five years not only has knitwear been a crucial part of the collections of high-fashion designers, but young people have taken up knitting with huge enthusiasm—both contributing to a more modern knitting design aesthetic. I do concede, however, that hand knits can sometimes look a little frumpy, so an awareness of trends and fashion directions can make the difference between a cabled sweater looking classic or catwalk.

Twice a year I go to the Pitti Filati trade show in Florence to see the new yarns, shades, color palette and trends predicted for the following year. I don't want to be a slavish follower of fashion, and I want to stay true to my own style, but I need to be aware of fashion forecasts to give the designs a contemporary feel. This is not just to cater to young knitters, as even my 93-year-old mother will ask me what colors or skirt lengths are "in."

The beauty of knitted fabric lies in its adaptability to the body, so use it to enhance your good points and hide your flaws.

A simple vent gives ease around the lower back.

A flat rib that becomes a cable and a change to a smaller needle will bring the fabric in.

designing for the body

So when designing for women, I want to combine the following elements: shapes that are flattering, styles that are in keeping with the current mood and fabrics that work with the yarn.

Proportion is crucial to me; it is inherent in anything I design. When I'm doing a workshop or presentation in a store, I always emphasize the importance of keeping to gauge. When I ask knitters if they work a square before each project, they usually look rather guilty or tell me that "their tension is always perfect(!)" But all yarns behave in different ways—an aran weight produced by one company may have a different construction from another—and this may affect your gauge. Different types of needles can alter how you knit, and even the mood you are in can play a part. A certain stitch pattern may affect the way you knit, too—you may become a looser knitter when working cables, for example—so don't take your gauge for granted! It's never an exact science—if you have a large number of stitches on the needle and the fabric is quite heavy, as when knitting an afghan, your gauge may be different than the swatch you worked up. Any difference from the stitches and rows quoted in the pattern will mean that the length and width of the finished garment will be different from that intended by the designer, and you won't end up with the same knit you saw and liked. Remember: Always check your gauge.

When looking at shapes, I aim to find pleasing proportions. A slim sleeve on a wide, boxy body will look strange and be uncomfortable to wear, as would loose-fitting sleeves or too deep an armhole on a slim silhouette. My goal is finding harmony and balance within a design. Any committed professional designer will put a lot of thought into the shape they are creating, so if your knitting doesn't match the given gauge, you will have altered the original intention. This is particularly true if the pattern quotes the length required, as you will have worked to the correct

length, but if you are a tight knitter, your garment will be narrower, potentially creating a too-lean look, plus the armholes and shoulders won't fit properly. I understand the excitement at starting a project, but you will have sacrificed the fit for fifteen minutes well spent beforehand. Have patience; it will be rewarded.

It is not just the aesthetics of a design that are important to me, but also how it sits on the body. A jacket or sweater that ends just across the widest part of your rear is not very flattering; neither is a long tunic that is tight across the hips. Obviously we all have different body shapes and waist-to-hip ratios, but by keeping to my general rules I hope to create the most pleasing shapes that are easy to wear.

As a traditional British pear shape, I avoid certain styles and am particularly aware of the hips when designing longer lines. To make sure there is ease in this area, I like to introduce some flare. This can be done in a variety of ways—for example, simple side shaping, working in a side or back vent as in **swatch A**, introducing cables to ribbing as in **swatch B**, decreasing between cables as in **swatch C**, or decreasing the size of the cables as in the Trapeze Coat (page 26). Smaller versions of swatch C can also be worked around a lower edge to create a peplumed effect. If the garment is a longer style with no shaping, it is better to have an unstructured hem rather than a rib that pulls in (or the rib should be knitted on the same-size needle as the body, rather than one or two needle sizes down). The A-line shape is perfect for the A-line body.

One of my most memorable moments was at a presentation I was doing at a store in the U.S. A woman tried on a generous jacket in my Donegal tweed yarn and looked fantastic in it. She seemed to grow in confidence as she twirled in it in front of the other customers. Later she confided in me that she hadn't knitted for herself for years because she feared that not only would she not find something that fit her

Decreasing
between the cables

C

larger size, but also that somehow she didn't deserve to make something that she could wear. She went away with the yarn for three projects that she knew she would look great in.

Larger women with bigger busts have a tendency to wear knits that are rather shapeless, which consequently makes their bodies look shapeless too. A bit of subtle tailoring can work wonders on plus sizes and create a waist where one doesn't exist. A larger bust can look matronly in a loose sweater, but A-line shapes that flare just under the bust can make a larger woman look like a Italian starlet, as can scoop necks, wide '50s-style collars, and V-necks.

A word here about sizing. One of the most

rewarding things for me is to take trunk shows around to the stores so that customers can try the knits on. I always think it's a huge leap of faith when a knitter buys a pattern and yarn to knit a design that she has only seen pictured on a model. What great optimists we knitters are, tackling projects that may take weeks to complete without knowing until that final moment when we sew it up whether it fits or not! No wonder so many knitters tell me that they have lots of unfinished projects lying around waiting to be sewn up; they're putting off the final moment of completion.

It can be a revelation to me at a trunk show to see how different the designs look depending on who is wearing them—how they change with body shape and

designing for the body

personality. Time and again I meet women who think they won't fit into my samples, which are usually size 34" bust. Reluctantly (I can be very persuasive!) they will try one on and be amazed that not only does it fit, but that if it is too small, they need only go up one size. Larger women often make knits that are too big, forgetting that the knitted fabric is a forgiving one that will stretch and mold—a size-38 woman may need to make a size 36 to fit properly on her shoulders. Checking the actual measurements of the garment in the pattern as well as the bust size will work wonders.

Designers are sometimes accused of being body fascists when they don't always grade a pattern up to larger sizes, but there is often a good reason why a design isn't available in a size 46" bust and beyond. I like to compare it to shoes: I may see a style in the window that looks perfect, but when I see the same style in my size something seems to have been lost. Some shapes, a bolero for example, will not have the same appeal in a larger size because as all the measurements change, the essential elements and proportions have changed and the knitter will be disappointed with the finished project. When I feel that the integrity of the design won't be compromised, I will grade up to as many sizes as possible. Also some large stitch repeats are not workable in a wide range of sizes, which is why knitting patterns sometimes have

what seems to be illogical sizing, such as to fit 32"–34" inch and 38"–40" chests, with no middle size.

I should mention the smaller sizes too, of course. As someone who, until I had my children, had the body shape of Olive Oyl (but without the advantage of her height), I know that being skinny doesn't always mean that knits will flatter. I find that tailored knits suit me better than casual styles, and generous sweaters swamp my shoulders.

The other factor I keep in mind when designing is the nature of the yarn. I like to imagine that the yarn tells me how to design. It's true that, with my own brand of yarns, I get to research and develop the fibers that interest me as a knitter, which gives me an advantage as a designer, but the fiber always inspires the garment. If a yarn has drape, as in my bamboo/wool blend, Prima, it will make me create shapes where the fabric can flow or skim the body. I prefer to think simple with yarns that drape in order to keep the swing true and let the yarn speak. Prima is perfect for dresses or tunics because the bamboo gives it lightness and sheen and the wool imparts elasticity. My Cashmerino mixes are soft and snuggly, just right for baby garments and knits with cozy collars, and my extra-fine merino, Rialto, has so much bounce (it is the Tigger of fibers!) that it lends itself to sporty tops and patterns that need clarity of stitch. ■

If you are interested in creating a design for yourself using shaping details:

▶ Try a classic sweater on, pinch it in at the waist, and take a good, hard look in the mirror. Would it look better if there was a bit of waist shaping? Would a lower neckline be more flattering?

▶ Look at a simple pattern that you have, and see if you can make some adjustments, perhaps decreasing from the hem to the waist and then increasing out to the armholes for some waist shaping, adding flare to a longer style by casting on more stitches at the bottom and decreasing to the waist or under the bust.

▶ There are also ways to work with existing stitches to create effects. A simple flat rib can be drawn in at the waist by cabling the rib and changing to a smaller needle.

patterns

The three projects here show different elements of body shaping.

Garter Stitch Coat

This coat is beautifully simple and easy to knit. The reversible fabric means that the collar just lies back over the body and there are no unattractive seams showing or picked-up bands. The shaping and length create a loose fitting coat with a flattering swing that suits all body shapes. Knitted in Rialto, my extra fine merino in an aran weight, it still is a lightweight coat, perfect for all seasons.

Ribbed Jacket

This simple ribbed jacket is enhanced by adding a decorative tie and a large button. Because there aren't any other buttons down the center, the fronts don't pull across the body over the bust, and a diagonal line is created. It is very easy to knit and very wearable—perfect as a cover-up when the temperatures start to drop. The yarn, Cashmerino Aran, molds to the body in the ribbed pattern and makes a waist, where a waist may not exist! Ribs are a great stitch to use to create shape other than making shaping by increasing and decreasing in the fabric.

Trapeze Coat

Here you get a design in my favorite shape, the A-line. There is no hem at the lower edge of the design, so it doesn't pull in, and the unstructured edge lends added detail. The cables are decreased up from the hem from large cables to much smaller ones. The sleeves become part of the yoke and are sewn to the flared body so that the garment has both vertical and horizontal patterning. The rows of cables at the point where the body meets the yoke define the empire line. A large cable at the back travels up to form part of the back yoke, and the scoop neck adds simplicity to an intricately patterned design.

Garter Stitch Coat

A graceful swing coat with slightly flared sleeves and a face-framing wide collar. Knitted in garter stitch, it's so easy to wear that I have two in different colors!

TO FIT BUST
81–86, 92–97, 102–107, 112–117 cm
32–34, 36–38, 40–42, 44–46 in

FINISHED MEASUREMENTS
BUST
90, 101, 112, 123 cm
35½, 39¾, 44, 48½ in

LENGTH TO SHOULDER
70, 72, 74, 76 cm
27½, 28¼, 29¼, 30 in

SLEEVE LENGTH
44, 44, 45, 45 cm
17¼, 17¼, 17¾, 17¾ in

MATERIALS
● 21 (22, 24, 25) 50g balls of Debbie Bliss Rialto Aran in Charcoal 26.
● Pair of 5mm (US 8) knitting needles.

TENSION
■ 18 sts and 36 rows to 10cm/4in square over garter st using 5mm (US 8) needles.

ABBREVIATIONS
See page 123.

BACK
With 5mm (US 8) needles, cast on 145 (155, 165, 175) sts.
K 5 (7, 9, 11) rows.
1st dec row (right side) K14 (15, 16, 17), skpo, k40 (43, 46, 49), k2tog, k29 (31, 33, 35), skpo, k40 (43, 46, 49), k2tog, k14 (15, 16, 17).
K 9 rows.
2nd dec row (right side) K14 (15, 16, 17), skpo, k38 (41, 44, 47), k2tog, k29 (31, 33, 35), skpo, k38 (41, 44, 47), k2tog, k14 (15, 16, 17).
K 9 rows.
3rd dec row (right side) K14 (15, 16, 17), skpo, k36 (39, 42, 45), k2tog, k29 (31, 33, 35), skpo, k36 (39, 42, 45), k2tog, k14 (15, 16, 17).
K 9 rows.
Cont in this way to dec 4 sts on next row and 12 foll 10th rows. 81 (91, 101, 111) sts.
Cont straight until back measures 46 (47, 48, 49)cm/ 18 (18½, 19, 19¼)in from cast on edge, ending with a wrong side row.
Shape armholes
Cast off 4 (5, 6, 7) sts at beg of next 2 rows.
73 (81, 89, 97) sts.
Next row K2, skpo, k to last 4 sts, k2tog, k2.
Next row K to end.
Rep the last 2 rows 7 (8, 9, 10) times more.
57 (63, 69, 75) sts.
Cont in garter st until back measures 70 (72, 74, 76)cm/27½ (28¼, 29¼, 30) in from cast on edge, ending with a wrong side row.
Shape shoulders
Cast off 7 (8, 9, 10) sts at beg of next 4 rows.
Cast off rem 29 (31, 33, 35) sts.

Garter Stitch Coat

LEFT FRONT

With 5mm (US 8) needles, cast on 87 (93, 99, 105) sts.
K 5 (7, 9, 11) rows.

1st dec row (right side) K14 (15, 16, 17), skpo,
k40 (43, 46, 49), k2tog, k29 (31, 33, 35).
K 9 rows.

2nd dec row (right side) K14 (15, 16, 17), skpo,
k38 (41, 44, 47), k2tog, k29 (31, 33, 35).
K 9 rows.

3rd dec row (right side) K14 (15, 16, 17), skpo,
k36 (39, 42, 45), k2tog, k29 (31, 33, 35).
K 9 rows.

Cont in this way to dec 2 sts on next row and 12 foll 10th
rows. 55 (61, 67, 73) sts.

Cont straight until front measures 46 (47, 48, 49)cm/18 (18½, 19,
19¼) in from cast on edge, ending with a wrong side row.

Shape armhole

Next row Cast off 4 (5, 6, 7) sts, k to end. 51 (56, 61, 66) sts.

Next row K to end.

Next row K2, skpo, k to end.

Next row K to end.

Rep the last 2 rows 7 (8, 9, 10) times more. 43 (47, 51, 55) sts.
Cont in garter st until front measures 70 (72, 74, 76)cm/27½ (28¼,

29¼, 30) in from cast on edge, ending with a wrong side row.

Shape shoulder

Cast off 7 (8, 9, 10) sts at beg of next row and foll right side row.
K 1 row.
Leave rem 29 (31, 33, 35) sts on a spare needle.

RIGHT FRONT

With 5mm (US 8) needles, cast on 87 (93, 99, 105) sts.
K 5 (7, 9, 11) rows.

1st dec row (right side) K29 (31, 33, 35), skpo,
k40 (43, 46, 49), k2tog, k14 (15, 16, 17).
K 9 rows.

2nd dec row (right side) K29 (31, 33, 35), skpo,
k38 (41, 44, 47), k2tog, k14 (15, 16, 17).
K 9 rows.

3rd dec row (right side) K29 (31, 33, 35), skpo,
k36 (39, 42, 45), k2tog, k14 (15, 16, 17).
K 9 rows.

Cont in this way to dec 2 sts on next row and 12 foll 10th rows.
55 (61, 67, 73) sts.

Cont straight until front measures 46 (47, 48, 49)cm/
18 (18½, 19, 19¼) in from cast on edge, ending with a
right side row.

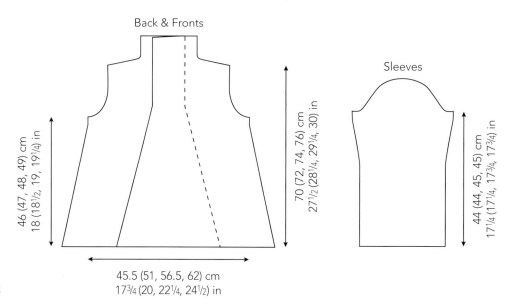

Back & Fronts

46 (47, 48, 49) cm
18 (18½, 19, 19¼) in

70 (72, 74, 76) cm
27½ (28¼, 29¼, 30) in

45.5 (51, 56.5, 62) cm
17¾ (20, 22¼, 24½) in

Sleeves

44 (44, 45, 45) cm
17¼ (17¼, 17¾, 17¾) in

Garter Stitch Coat

Shape armhole
Next row Cast off 4 (5, 6, 7) sts, k to end. 51 (56, 61, 66) sts.
Next row K to last 4 sts, k2tog, k2.
Next row K to end.
Rep the last 2 rows 7 (8, 9, 10) times more. 43 (47, 51, 55) sts.
Cont in garter st until front measures 70 (72, 74, 76)cm/27½ (28¼, 29¼, 30) in from cast on edge, ending with a right side row.

Shape shoulder
Cast off 7 (8, 9, 10) sts at beg of next row and foll wrong side row, leave rem 29 (31, 33, 35) sts on needle.

COLLAR
With 5mm (US 8) needles, k across 29 (31, 33, 35) sts from right front, cast on 39 (42, 45, 48) sts, k across 29 (31, 33, 35) sts from left front. 97 (104, 111, 118) sts.
Work in garter st until collar measures 15cm/6in.
Cast off.

SLEEVES
With 5mm (US 8) needles, cast on 60 (64, 68, 72) sts.
K 69 (69, 73, 73) rows.
Next row (right side) K4, m1, k to last 4 sts, m1, k4.
K 11 rows.
Rep the last 12 rows 3 times more and the inc row again. 70 (74, 78, 82) sts.
Cont straight until sleeve measures 44 (44, 45, 45)cm/17¼ (17¼, 17¾, 17¾) in from cast-on edge, ending with a wrong side row.

Shape top
Cast off 4 (5, 6, 7) sts at beg of next 2 rows. 62 (64, 66, 68) sts.
Next row K2, skpo, k to last 4 sts, k2tog, k2.
Next row K to end.
Rep the last 2 rows 7 (8, 9, 10) times more. 46 sts.
K 2 rows.
Next row K2, skpo, k to last 4 sts, k2tog, k2.
Next row K to end.
Rep the last 4 rows 7 times more. 30 sts.
Cast off 3 sts at beg of next 6 rows.
Cast off rem 12 sts.

TO MAKE UP
Join shoulder seams. Sew cast on sts of collar to back neck edge, easing to fit. Sew sleeves into armholes, easing to fit. Join side and sleeve seams. ✤

Ribbed Jacket

A so-simple top that molds to the body to make a form-fitting jacket.

TO FIT BUST

81–86, 92–97, 102–107, 112–117 cm

32–34, 36–38, 40–42, 44–46in

FINISHED MEASUREMENTS

BUST

92, 102, 112, 123 cm

36, 40, 44, 48½ in

LENGTH TO SHOULDER

51, 53, 55, 57 cm

20, 21, 21¾, 22½ in

SLEEVE LENGTH

44, 45, 46, 47 cm

17¼, 17¾, 18, 18½ in

MATERIALS

● 11 (12, 13, 14) 50g balls of Debbie Bliss Cashmerino DK in Peach 23.
● Pair size 4mm (US 6) knitting needles.
● Pair size 3.75mm (US 5) knitting needles.
● One large button.
● 20cm/8in suede strip.

TENSION

■ 23 sts and 32 rows to 10cm/4in square over rib patt when slightly stretched using 4mm (US 6) needles.

ABBREVIATIONS

See page 123.

BACK

With 4mm (US 6) needles, cast on 107 (119, 131, 143) sts.

1st row (right side) K2, [p1, k2] to end.

2nd row P2, [k1, p2] to end.

These 2 rows form the patt and are repeated.

Work straight until back measures 31 (32, 33, 34)cm/12¼ (12½, 13, 13¼) in from cast on edge, ending with a wrong side row.

Shape armholes

Cast off 5 sts at beg of next 2 rows. 97 (109, 121, 133) sts.

Keeping patt correct cont straight until back measures 51 (53, 55, 57)cm/20 (21, 21¾, 22½) in from cast on edge, ending with a wrong side row.

Shape shoulders

Cast off 30 (33, 39, 42) sts at beg of next 2 rows.

Leave rem 37 (43, 43, 49) sts on a holder for collar.

LEFT FRONT

With 4mm (US 6) needles, cast on 71 (80, 86, 95) sts.

1st row (right side) K2, [p1, k2] to end.

2nd row P2, [k1, p2] to end.

These 2 rows form the patt and are repeated.

Work straight until front measures 31 (32, 33, 34)cm/12¼ (12½, 13, 13¼)in from cast on edge, ending with a wrong side row.

Shape armhole

Next row Cast off 5 sts, patt to end. 66 (75, 81, 90) sts.

Keeping patt correct cont straight until front measures 39 (41, 43, 45)cm/15¼ (16, 17, 17¾) in from cast on edge, ending with a wrong side row.

Shape neck

Next row (right side) Patt 48 (54, 57, 63), turn and cont on these sts only, leave rem 18 (21, 24, 27) sts on a holder.

Cast off 4 sts at beg (neck edge) of next row and 2 sts at beg of foll 4 (6, 4, 6) wrong side rows.

Patt 3 rows.

Cont in patt and dec 1 st at neck edge on next row and foll 5 (4, 5, 4) 4th rows. 30 (33, 39, 42) sts.

Cont straight in patt until front matches Back to shoulder, ending at armhole edge.

Cast off for shoulder.

Ribbed Jacket

RIGHT FRONT

With 4mm (US 6) needles, cast on 71 (80, 86, 95) sts.

1st row (right side) K2, [p1, k2] to end.

2nd row P2, [k1, p2] to end.

These 2 rows form the patt and are repeated.

Work straight until front measures 31 (32, 33, 34)cm/12¼ (12½, 13, 13¼) in from cast on edge, ending with a right side row.

Shape armhole

Next row Cast off 5 sts, patt to end. 66 (75, 81, 90) sts.

Cont straight in patt until front measures 39 (41, 43, 45)cm/15¼ (16, 17, 17¾) in from cast on edge, ending with a wrong side row.

Shape neck

Next row (right side) Patt 18 (21, 24, 27) sts and slip these sts onto a holder, cast off next 4 sts, patt to end and cont on these 44 (50, 53, 59) sts only.

Patt 1 row.

Cast off 2 sts at beg of foll 4 (6, 4, 6) right side rows.

Patt 3 rows.

Cont in patt and dec 1 st at neck edge on next row and foll 5 (4, 5, 4) 4th rows. 30 (33, 39, 42) sts.

Cont straight in patt until front matches Back to shoulder, ending at armhole edge.

Cast off for shoulder.

SLEEVES

With 4mm (US 6) needles, cast on 47 (50, 53, 56) sts.

1st row (right side) K2, [p1, k2] to end.

2nd row P2, [k1, p2] to end.

These 2 rows form the patt and are repeated.

Patt a further 10 (10, 6, 6) rows.

Cont in patt and inc 1 st at each end of next row and every foll 5th row, taking all inc sts into patt, until there are 95 (98, 107, 110) sts.

Cont straight in patt until sleeve measures 44 (45, 46, 47)cm/17¼ (17¾, 18, 18½) in from cast on edge, place a marker at each end of last row, then work a further 8 (8, 12, 12) rows.

Cast off in patt.

COLLAR

With right side facing and 4mm (US 6) needles, slip 18 (21, 24, 27) sts from right front holder onto a needle, pick up and k 41 sts up right front neck, patt across 37 (43, 43, 49) sts of back neck, pick up and k 41 sts down left front neck, then patt across 18 (21, 24, 27) sts from left front holder. 155 (167, 173, 185) sts.

Change to 3.75mm (US 5) needles.

1st row (wrong side) P2, [k1, p2] to end.

2nd row K2, [p1, k2] to end.

These 2 rows form the patt and are repeated.

Cont in patt until collar measures 14cm/5½ in from pick up row.

Cast off in patt.

TO MAKE UP

With center of cast off edge of sleeve to shoulder, sew sleeves into armholes with row ends above markers sewn to sts cast off at underarm. Join side and sleeve seams. Fold suede strip in half and attach fold to edge of right front, sew large button in place on left front to match. ✽

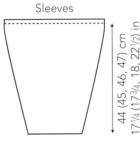

Back & Fronts

31 (32, 33, 34) cm
12¼ (12¾, 13, 13¼) in

51 (53, 55, 57) cm
20 (21, 21¾, 22½) in

46.5 (51.5, 57, 62) cm
18¼ (20¼, 22¼, 24½) in

Sleeves

44 (45, 46, 47) cm
17¼ (17¾, 18, 22½) in

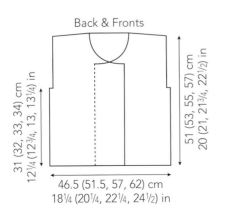

Trapeze Coat

This A-line coat is made special by its multi-textured patterning.

TO FIT BUST
81–86, 92–97, 102–107 cm
32–34, 36–38, 40–42 in

FINISHED MEASUREMENTS
BUST
88, 99, 110 cm
34¾, 39, 43¼ in

LENGTH TO SHOULDER
64, 68, 73 cm
25¼, 26¾, 28¾ in

SLEEVE LENGTH
43, 45, 47 cm
17, 17¾, 18½ in

MATERIALS
● 19 (20, 21) 50g balls of
Debbie Bliss Cashmerino
Aran in Stone 102
● Pair 5mm (US 8) knitting
needles
● Long 4.5mm (US 7) and 5mm
(US 8) circular needles
● Cable needle
● 4 buttons

TENSION
■ 18 sts and 24 rows to
10cm/4in square over st st
and 14.5 sts and 28 rows to
10cm/4in square over 4-st
cable patt, both using 5mm
(US 8) needles

PATTERN A
(Worked over 6 sts)
1st row (right side) P1, C4F, p1.
2nd row K1, p4, k1.
3rd row P1, k4, p1.
4th row As 2nd row.
These 4 rows form patt A and are repeated.

PATTERN B
(Worked over 8 sts)
1st row (right side) K1, p2, k2, p2, k1.
2nd row K2, p2, k2, p2.
3rd row P1, k2, p2, k2, p1.
4th row P2, k2, p2, k2.
These 4 rows form patt B and are repeated.

PATTERN C
(Worked over 18 sts, dec to 15 sts, dec to 12 sts,
dec to 9 sts, dec to 6 sts)
1st row (right side) K18.
2nd and every foll wrong side row P to end.
3rd row K6, C12F.
5th, 7th, 9th and 11th rows K18.
13th row C12B, k6.
15th, 17th and 19th rows K18.
21st to 38th rows Rep 1st to 18th rows.
39th (dec) row K3, [k2tog, k3] 3 times. 15 sts.
40th row P15.
41st row K5, C10F.
43rd, 45th and 47th rows K15.
49th row C10B, k5.
51st, 53rd and 55th rows K15.
56th to 68th rows Rep 40th to 52nd rows.
69th (dec) row K3, [k2tog, k2] 3 times. 12 sts.
70th row P12.
71st row K4, C8F.
73rd and 75th rows K12.
77th row C8B, k4.

Trapeze Coat

79th and **81st rows** K12.
82nd to **90th rows** Rep 70th to 78th rows.
91st (dec) row K1, [k2tog, k2] twice, k2tog, k1. 9 sts.
92nd row P9.
93rd row K3, C6F.
95th row K9.
97th row C6B, k3.
99th row K9.
100th to **106th rows** Rep 92nd to 98th rows.
107th (dec) row [K2tog, k1] 3 times. 6 sts.
108th row P6.
109th row K2, C4F.
110th row P6.
111th row C4B, k2.
112th row P6.
The last 4 rows only (109–112) are repeated.

PATTERN D

(Worked over 23 sts)
1st row (right side) P1, k2, p4, C4F, p1, C4B, p4, k2, p1.
2nd row K1, p2, k4, p4, k1, p4, k4, p2, k1.
3rd row P1, C4FP, p2, k4, p1, k4, p2, C4BP, p1.
4th row K3, p2, k2, p4, k1, p4, k2, p2, k3.
5th row P3, C4F, C4FP, p1, C4BP, C4B, p3.
6th row K3, p4, k2, p2, k1, p2, k2, p4, k3.
7th row P1, C4BP, C4FP, k2, p1, k2, C4BP, C4FP, p1.
8th row K1, p2, k4, p4, k1, p4, k4, p2, k1.
These 8 rows form patt D and are repeated.

PATTERN E

(Worked over 6 sts)
1st row (right side) P1, C4B, p1.
2nd row K1, p4, k1.
3rd row P1, k4, p1.
4th row As 2nd row.
These 4 rows form patt E and are repeated.

PATTERN F

(Worked over 8 sts)
1st row (right side) K1, p2, k2, p2, k1.
2nd row P2, k2, p2, k2.
3rd row P1, k2, p2, k2, p1.
4th row K2, p2, k2, p2.
These 4 rows form patt F and are repeated.

FRONTS AND BACK

With 5mm (US 8) circular needle, cast on 365 (409, 453) sts.
Foundation row (wrong side) [P1, k1] 3 times, p1, pfb, p1, k3, p2, k2, p2, k1, p1, pfb, p1, k2, p2, [k2, p5, pfb, p4, pfb, p5, k2, p2] 6 (7, 8) times, k2, p1, pfb, p1, k3, p2, k2, p2, k1, p2, k4, p1, pfb, p1, k1, p1, pfb, p1, k4, p2, k1, p2, k2, p2, k3, p1, pfb, p1, k2, [p2, k2, p5, pfb, p4, pfb, p5, k2] 6 (7, 8) times, p2, k2, p1, pfb, p1, k1, p2, k2, p2, k3, p1, pfb, p1, [k1, p1] 3 times. 397 (445, 493) sts.
1st row (right side) P1, [k1, p1] twice, work 1st row of patts A, B and A, p1, [Tw2R, p2, work 1st row of patt C, p2] 6 (7, 8) times, Tw2R, p1, work 1st row of patts A, B, D, F and E, p1, Tw2R, [p2, work 1st row of patt C, p2, Tw2R] 6 (7, 8) times, p1, work 1st row of patts E, F and E, [p1, k1] twice, p1.
2nd row P1, [k1, p1] twice, work 2nd row of patts E, F and E, k1, [p2, k2, work 2nd row of patt C, k2] 6 (7, 8) times, p2, k1, work 2nd row of patts E, F, D, B and A, k1, p2, [k2, work 2nd row of patt C, k2, p2] 6 (7, 8) times, k1, work 2nd row of patts A, B and A, [p1, k1] twice, p1.
These 2 rows set the position of the patt panels and form twisted sts and moss st front edges and are repeated working correct patt panel rows and working decreases as given within patt C.
When all decreases have been worked, 253 (277, 301) sts rem.
Cont straight in patts as set until work measures 43 (46, 49)cm/17 (18, 19¼)in, ending with a right side row.
(See Note for measuring length)
Next row (wrong side) Patt 30 and slip these sts onto a holder for Right Front, cast off next 66 (78, 90) sts, then with one st on needle after cast off, patt next 60 sts and slip these 61 sts onto a holder for Back, cast off next 66 (78, 90) sts, patt to end.

RIGHT FRONT

With 5mm (US 8) needles, cont in patt as set on first group of 30 sts.

Buttonhole row (right side) P1, k1, yf, k2tog, p1, patt to end.
Patt 13 (15, 15) rows.

Buttonhole row (right side) P1, k1, yf, k2tog, p1, patt to end.
Rep the last 14 (16, 16) rows twice more.
Patt 3 (1, 5) rows, so ending with a wrong side row.

Shape neck

Next row (right side) Patt 11 and slip these sts onto a holder for neck edge, cast off 3 sts, patt to end.
Patt 1 row.
Cont in patt and cast off 3 sts at beg of next row, 2 sts at beg of next 3 right side rows and one st at beg of foll right side row.
Patt 3 rows.
Cast off rem 6 sts.

CENTER BACK PANEL

With right side facing and 5mm (US 8) needles, rejoin yarn to 61 sts on Back holder.
Cont in patt as set and work a further 59 (63, 67) rows.

Shape shoulders

Next row Cast off 6 sts, patt to last 6 sts, cast off these 6 sts.
Leave rem 49 sts on a holder.

LEFT FRONT

With right side facing and 5mm (US 8) needles, rejoin yarn to 30 sts on Left Front holder.
Work 46 (50, 54) rows in patt as set.

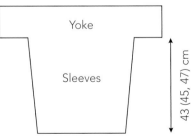

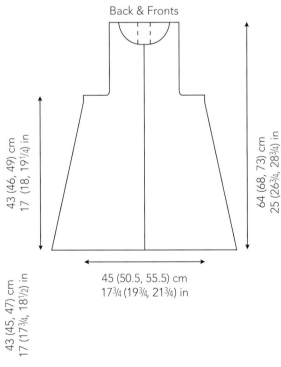

Back & Fronts

43 (46, 49) cm
17 (18, 19¼) in

64 (68, 73) cm
25 (26¾, 28¾) in

45 (50.5, 55.5) cm
17¾ (19¾, 21¾) in

Yoke

Sleeves

43 (45, 47) cm
17 (17¾, 18½) in

Trapeze Coat

Shape neck

Next row (right side) Patt to last 11 sts, turn and leave these sts on a holder.

Cast off 3 sts at beg (neck edge) of next row and foll wrong side row, then 2 sts at beg of next 3 wrong side rows and one st at beg of foll wrong side row. 6 sts.

Patt 2 rows.

Cast off.

SLEEVES

With 5mm (US 8) needles, cast on 47 sts.

Foundation row (wrong side) K1, p1, pfb, p1, k3, p2, k2, p2, k1, p2, k4, p1, pfb, p1, k1, p1, pfb, p1, k4, p2, k1, p2, k2, p2, k3, p1, pfb, p1, k1. 51 sts.

Now work in patt as follows:

1st row (right side) Work 1st rows of patts A, B, D, F and E.

2nd row Work 2nd rows of patts E, F, D, B and A.

These 2 rows set the position of the patt panels.

Working correct patt panel rows, work a further 4 rows, then inc 1 st at each end of next row and 7 foll 4th rows, taking inc sts into patt panels F at beg and B at end of right side rows, then inc 1 st at each end of every foll 6th row, taking first 6 sts at each side into patt panels E at beg and A at end of right side rows and rem inc sts into patt panels B at beg and F at end of right side rows until there are 95 sts.

Cont straight until sleeve measures approximately 43 (45, 47)cm/17 (17¾, 18½)in (measured along 4 st cable) from cast on edge, ending with a 2nd row of patts A and E.

Change to 5mm (US 8) circular needle.

Shape yoke

Next row (right side) Cast on 16 (21, 26) sts and work, p1, [k4, p1] 3 (4, 5) times across these sts, patt to end.

Next row Cast on 16 (21, 26) sts, k1, [p4, k1] 3 (4, 5) times across these sts, patt to last 16 sts, k1, [p4, k1] 3 times. 127 sts.

Next row P1, [C4B, p1] 3 (4, 5) times, patt to last 16 sts, [p1, C4F] 3 (4, 5) times, p1.

The last row sets the position of the 3 (4, 5) 4-st cables to each side of the center patt panels.

Cont to work a further 28 (32, 36) rows in patts, working cables on every 4th row, so ending with a right side cable row.

Cast off, working 2 sts tog in center of each 4-st cable including Patt D.

NECKBAND

Join 6 sts of fronts to back at either side of neck shaping along shoulder line.

With right side facing and 4.5mm (US 7) needles, slip 11 sts from right front holder onto needle, pick up and k24 sts up right front neck, k across 49 sts at center back, pick up and k24 sts down left front neck, then patt across 11 sts from left front holder. 119 sts.

Dec row (wrong side) Patt 11, p1, [k1, p1] 12 times, k2tog, [p1, k1] 9 times, p2tog, k1, p1, k1, p2tog, [k1, p1] 9 times, k2tog, [p1, k1] 12 times, p1, patt 11. 115 sts.

Next row Patt 11, [k1, p1] 41 times, patt 11.

Rep the last row once more.

Cast off in patt and moss st, working k2tog across center 2 sts of each 4-st cable.

TO MAKE UP

Join sleeve seams and yoke cast on edges. With center of cast off edge of sleeve/yoke to shoulder line, sew to back and front yoke edges, then sew row ends of yoke to cast off edges of back/fronts. Sew on buttons. ✲

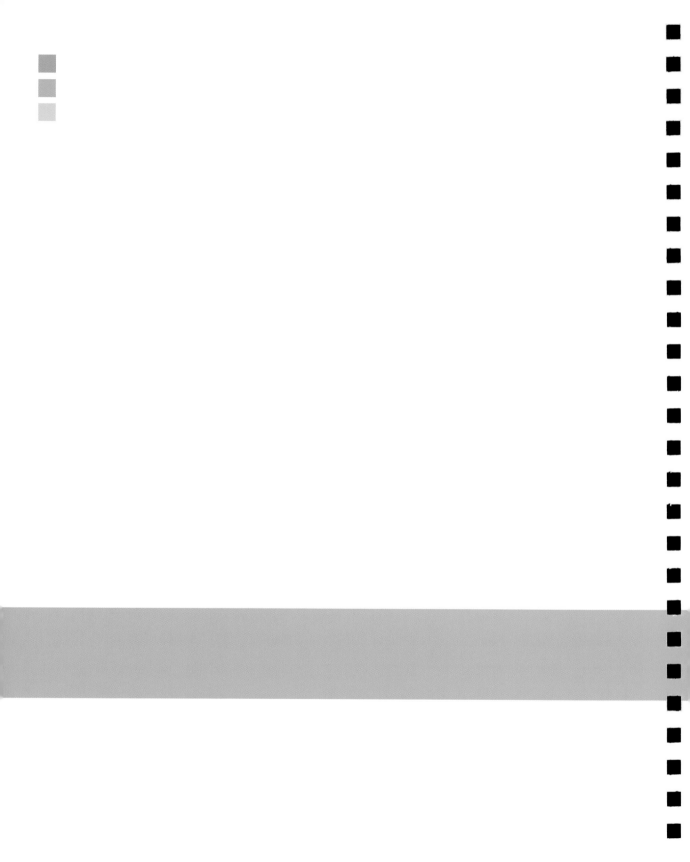

2:designing with color

designing with color

Color has a tremendous influence on all of us. It can relax us, comfort us, excite us or inspire us. My first color memory is going to see Walt Disney's *Sleeping Beauty*. There was a moment when the shades of the dresses of the fairy godmothers magically changed, and I felt elated as I watched. Color still has this power to affect me.

Certain color combinations are very evocative to me. Earthy terracotta with gold and intense blue is the palette not only of the ancient Minoans and Greeks but also the Native Americans, cultures that all fascinate me. Sage green and magenta pink with off-white

remind me of faded English chintz and afternoon tea. I also love to combine colors that should clash, such as crimson with fuchsia.

My first commissioned design was a color project. The jacket was designed based on a painting by Sonia Delauney, a Modernist painter active in the 1920s whose work combined vivid swirls of color with geometrics. Thirty years later, I still have the chunky jacket I knitted for this assignment. The intarsia pattern, which was a very strong look at the time, has since returned to fashion, and my daughter wears the jacket now.

When working with color the proportion of one shade to another is very important. I can have six or seven balls of yarn that I think will make a beautiful Fair Isle, but when I start swatching, I'm really disappointed with the result. Even if the swatch is working well, the next few rows can throw it into disarray, because the balance of color is wrong. If I had a pound for every Fair Isle swatch I've discarded, I would be a rich woman!

It's not easy finding the right color combinations. I've learned over the years not to attempt color swatching late at night. Too many times I've gone to bed convinced I've cracked a color sequence, only to wake the next day and find it doesn't work at all. When working **swatch A**, I initially tried a red that I thought would work well with the other colors, but

the shade seemed wrong—I changed to a very slightly brighter red, and the pattern came alive. The best way to see the interplay of colors is through Fair Isle, where the color changes are frequent.

Try experimenting with Fair Isles by taking one pattern and working it not only in different shades but also in different weights of yarn. A pastel pattern in a fine yarn can look completely different when swatched in vivid brights in a chunky weight. I'm always inspired when I see my Fair Isle sweater patterns worked in different colors. I am not at all offended when people use different colors than the ones I originally chose; I love the way that something I have designed has been transformed into something unique to the knitter.

When I am working on color pattern in a design I often like to introduce some color into the borders to pull everything together. In **swatch B** the shades in the Fair Isle yoke are echoed in the cast on stripe on the lower border, the ends of the split collar and on the finished garment, on the sleeve cuffs. By doing this I feel it creates a harmony in the design and I have used this effect in the Fair Isle Cardigan by color tipping the points of the picot edge.

When working stripes of color pacing and color choice are very important. Width of stripe, the balance of background to contrast colors all contribute to the dynamics of the design.

In the first repeat of the diamond and cross pattern there is a small amount of pink in the center of the pale grey. In the second repeat the diamonds and crosses are in the pink. By reversing the dominant color the pattern takes on a different dynamic.

Changing to a very slightly brighter red, and the pattern came alive. Lesson: Subtle color moves can make the difference between color patterning being successful or not.

The colors in the fairisle yoke are echoed on the inner edge of the body and on the collar. This creates a harmony in the design.

The proportion of one shade to another is very important.

designing with color

In **swatch C** I used contrast colors against a dark grey background. By winding off small amounts of the contrast colors that attracted me beforehand I found a sequence that I liked. I chose the following three shades of teal blue shading to duck egg, two shades of green, three shades of purple shading to lilac, two shades of blue, three shades of red shading to pink. The width of stripe narrowed as the colors became lighter and by shading the colors the stripes fade away giving a slightly more three dimensional quality to the pattern.
The whole sequence of stripes is then repeated.

In **swatch D** I wanted to stagger the color sequence to see what would happen to the dynamic of the colors. I reknitted the swatch in the same contrast color sequence, pink, teal blue, green, purple, etc., but started the next contrast color before working the background stripe. This produces for example a narrow green stripe ending the band of pale blue, a narrow purple stripe ending the band of green. As I continued in this way I could see how the different colors worked against each other without grey background separating them and also how these colors worked when a previously narrower stripe, the light pink for example, became wider. I also made the background narrower. As I kept on knitting every repeat brought a different combination and there was an endless permutation of patterning, so it was a great way to hit on a color juxtaposition that I may not have previously thought of.

Stripes like the ones pictured right are a great way to experiment with color knitting because they are

designing with color

simple to knit, and, since you don't have to worry about techniques such as intarsia or Fair Isle, you can concentrate on discovering good combinations and the balance of contrast against background. Fine color stripes can be achieved by working in garter stitch as every two rows look like one row and your background and contrast color will always begin at the same side of the work.

If you want to work very fine, one row, two color stripes in stockinette stitch so that you aren't constantly cutting the yarn to start again at the other end, try simply knitting them on double-pointed needles and working in the same direction for both stripes. (This is far easier to knit than to explain; try it, it works!)

When going into a yarn store, color's the first thing that I notice; it's what will draw me toward a particular yarn before I've even touched it to feel its weight or softness. One of the most exciting things for me when I visit a really good yarn store is to see the time and effort that has gone into displaying the yarns. Some store owners group yarns together by hue, which can be quite striking, but personally I like to see how shades work together.

In my own yarn brand I like to introduce new yarns, initially in twelve or sixteen shades, and I look for a color balance in the palette; naturally I always include some classics, such as ecru and stone. I take the time to get my sample shades together, arranging and rearranging them until I feel that there is harmony within the range. Sometimes a shade is needed to bring energy to it—for example a lime added to

chocolate browns and blues will often make them come alive. Color of course is very subjective, and we all have our favorites. People tease me that every range I create will include duck-egg blue, a soft pastel between blue and green that is my personal favorite. Every season, I introduce new shades into my existing yarns, and I need to be aware of trend colors. I couldn't introduce a color that I found really unattractive, but as with silhouettes and styles, those colors we may not like one season sometimes do grow on us after we see fashions made with them in stores.

When coming up with a color palette for a new yarn, I'm influenced by both the type of yarn and the season for its debut. I loved the softness of my Pure Cotton, which came out in Spring '07. Knitting up a swatch, I could only think of sorbet shades and chalky pastels. So I chose those kinds of colors, perfect for summer, for the yarn: raspberry, pistachio, melon and ice cream tones. Some of my spring yarns have silk in them; working with them turns my thoughts to the Far East—as a result, their colors are vibrant and vivid. With winter yarns, my mind immediately turns to smoky grays, berry shades and rustic hues.

I also love "hidden" color. This can work well in pockets or the underside of a collar or cuffs, as in the Tweed Jacket featured in this section. I particularly like it when used in children's designs, where a contrasting color in a pocket can be matched up in accompanying gloves or a hat. It can also be used on the underside of the hem, such as picot edge, or to "tip" an edge by picking up and casting off with another color around the edge of a decorative lace border. ■

There are a few techniques I prefer to use when working with color:

▶ Tipping (the knitting in of a bit of accent color) is something I love to do in my color designs. It may be as simple as introducing a cast-on or bind-off row on the ribbed bands in a contrast shade. This also works to frame the design, the same principle explored in the Texture (page 57) section.

▶ Introducing color to the borders pulls everything together.

▶ Sometimes I will introduce an alternating star pattern or stripes, or change from brights to pastels.

patterns

Three very different styles all show the impact of color.

Color Band Sweater

I love to use color banding, which is visible on this ribbed sweater with the deep rose, burnt orange and lime contrasting the dark green of the main body. These bands would look good against a stone shade, too. On this particular design I didn't include a picked-up neckband, because I wanted a really clean look with no interruption of the color. When changing color on a rib pattern there is a "dash" effect—an interrupted line between the two shades—that I don't like. To avoid this, I work a knit or purl row, whichever is appropriate, on the color change.

Favorite Fair Isle Cardigan

Here I used a classic stone shade for the background, which reminds me of the patterning in 1930s sweaters. I love the way that in traditional Fair Isles the contrast colors give a depth and three-dimensional quality to the patterning. This is what I did with the blues, while the red and lime highlight the diamond and star shapes and add vibrancy. Alternating the pink and red as the main shade in the diamonds creates a sense of the color receding and coming forward. An accent color tips each picot point.

Tweed Jacket with Contrast Lining

I also love "hidden" color, where the contrast is seen as a vivid flash. Tudor clothing for men used this technique, where the slashes in the outer fabric reveal the contrast color beneath. In this Tweed Jacket, the pocket lining and the inside of the turned-back cuffs and collar are worked in a bright magenta that is glimpsed as just a stripe. The tailored jacket could be seen as rather formal, so the slash of color contrasting against the lovely heathery tweed gives it some humor.

Color Band Sweater

The colorblock top with its wide neckline has a subtle yet sexy fit.

TO FIT BUST
81–86, 92–97, 102–107, 112–117 cm
32–34, 36–38, 40–42, 44–46 in

FINISHED MEASUREMENTS
(with rib stretched to fit)
BUST
87, 98, 109, 120 cm
34¼, 38½, 43, 47¼ in

LENGTH TO BACK NECK
47, 51, 55, 59 cm
18½, 20, 21¾, 23¼ in

SLEEVE LENGTH
45, 46, 47, 48 cm
17¾, 18, 18½, 19 in

MATERIALS
● 9 (10, 11, 12) 50g balls of
Debbie Bliss Baby Cashmerino in
Dark Olive Green 024 (A) and one 50g
ball in each of Rust 023 (B),
Pink 602 (C) and Lime 025 (D).
● Pair size 3.25mm (US 3) knitting
needles.
● One 3mm (US 2–3) circular
needle.

TENSION
■ 36 sts and 38 rows over rib patt
when left unstretched and 28 sts and
38 rows over rib patt when stretched
both to 10cm/4in square using
3.25mm (US 3) needles.

ABBREVIATIONS
See page 123.

BACK AND FRONT
(Both alike)
With 3.25mm (US 3) needles and B, cast on 125 (140,
155, 170) sts.
1st row (right side) P2, [k1, p2] to end.
2nd row K2, [p1, k2] to end.
These 2 rows form the rib patt and are repeated.
Cont in rib until work measures 6cm/2¼ in, ending with a 2nd row.
Change to A and k 1 row.
Beg with a 2nd row, cont in rib in A until work measures
31 (33, 35, 37)cm/12¼ (13, 13¾, 14½) in from cast on edge,
ending with a wrong side row.

Shape underarm and raglans
Cast off 6 sts in patt at beg of next 2 rows.
113 (128, 143, 158) sts.
Next row P2, skpo, patt to last 4 sts, k2tog, p2.
Next row K2, p1, patt to last 3 sts, p1, k2.
Rep the last 2 rows 6 (8, 10, 12) times more. 99 (110, 121, 132) sts.
Next row P2, k1, patt to last 3 sts, k1, p2.
Next row K2, p1, patt to last 3 sts, p1, k2.
Next row P2, skpo, patt to last 4 sts, k2tog, p2.
Next row K2, p1, patt to last 3 sts, p1, k2.
Rep the last 4 rows 6 (7, 8, 9) times more. 85 (94, 103, 112) sts.
Change to C and k 1 row.
Next row (wrong side) K2, p1, patt to last 3 sts, p1, k2.
Next row P2, skpo, patt to last 4 sts, k2tog, p2.
Next row K2, p1, patt to last 3 sts, p1, k2.
Next row P2, k1, patt to last 3 sts, k1, p2.
Rep the last 4 rows 2 times more, then work the first 3 of these
4 rows again. 77 (86, 95, 104) sts.
Leave sts on a holder.

SLEEVES
With 3.25mm (US 3) needles and D, cast on 59 (59, 65, 71) sts.
1st row (right side) P2, [k1, p2] to end.
2nd row K2, [p1, k2] to end.
These 2 rows form the rib patt and are repeated.

Color Band Sweater

Cont in rib until work measures 6cm/2¼in, ending with a 2nd row.

Change to A and k 1 row.

Beg with a 2nd row, cont in rib in A and inc 1 st at each end of next right side row and every foll 7th (6th, 7th, 7th) row taking all inc sts into rib patt until there are 95 (101, 107, 113 sts.

Cont straight in patt until sleeve measures 45(46, 47, 48)cm/17¾ (18, 18½, 19)in from cast on edge, ending with a wrong side row.

Shape underarm and raglan

Cast off 6 sts in patt at beg of next 2 rows. 83 (89, 95, 101) sts.

Next row (right side) P2, skpo, patt to last 4 sts, k2tog, p2.

Next row K2, p1, patt to last 3 sts, p1, k2.

Rep the last 2 rows 6 (8, 10, 12) times more. 69 (71, 73, 75) sts.

Next row (right side) P2, k1, patt to last 3 sts, k1, p2.

Next row K2, p1, patt to last 3 sts, p1, k2.

Next row P2, skpo, patt to last 4 sts, k2tog, p2.

Next row K2, p1, patt to last 3 sts, p1, k2.

Rep the last 4 rows 6 (7, 8, 9) times more. 55 sts.

Change to C and k 1 row.

Next row (wrong side) K2, p1, patt to last 3 sts, p1, k2.

Next row P2, skpo, patt to last 4 sts, k2tog, p2.

Next row K2, p1, patt to last 3 sts, p1, k2.

Next row P2, k1, patt to last 3 sts, k1, p2.

Rep the last 4 rows 2 times more, then work the first 3 of these 4 rows again. 47 sts.

Leave sts on a holder.

NECKBAND

Join raglan seams. With right side facing and 3mm (US 2-3) circular needle, work across sts from holders as follows: With C, p2tog, [k1, p2] 14 times, k1, p2tog across left sleeve, p2tog, [k1, p2] 24 (27, 30, 33) times, k1, p2tog across front, p2tog, [k1, p2] 14 times, k1, p2tog across right sleeve, then p2tog, [k1, p2] 24 (27, 30, 33) times, k1, p2tog across back. 240 (258, 276, 294) sts.

1st and 3rd sizes only

Cast off round Slip 1 (this st will be cast off at end of round), then cast off all sts as follows, * [k1, p2tog] 15 times, [k1, p2, k1, p2tog] 6(-, 7, -) times, k1, p2tog, [k1, p2, k1, p2tog] 6(-, 8, -) times, rep from * once more.

2nd and 4th sizes only

Cast off round Slip 1 (this st will be cast off at end of round), then cast off all sts as follows, [k1, p2tog] 15 times, [k1, p2, k1, p2tog] -(14, -, 17) times, [k1, p2tog] 15 times, [k1, p2, k1, p2tog] -(14, -, 17) times.

TO MAKE UP

Join side and sleeve seams. ❊

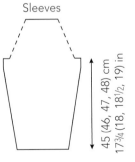

Sleeves

45 (46, 47, 48) cm
17¾ (18, 18½, 19) in

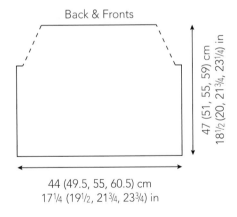

Back & Fronts

47 (51, 55, 59) cm
18½ (20, 21¾, 23¼) in

44 (49.5, 55, 60.5) cm
17¼ (19½, 21¾, 23¾) in

Fair Isle Cardigan

A sweet, feminine cardi in a classic Fair Isle with delicate picot edgings.

TO FIT BUST
81–86, 92–97, 102–107, 112–117 cm
32–34, 36–38, 40–42, 44–46 in

FINISHED MEASUREMENTS
BUST
93, 104, 116, 128 cm
36½, 41, 45½, 50½ in

LENGTH TO SHOULDER
50, 51, 52, 53 cm
19¾, 20, 20½, 21 in

SLEEVE LENGTH
30, 30, 31, 31 cm
12, 12, 12¼, 12¼ in

MATERIALS
● 4 (5, 5, 6) 50g balls of Debbie Bliss Baby Cashmerino in Silver 012 (M), 1 (2, 2, 2) 50g balls in each of Mid Blue 027 (A), Red 700 (B) and Pink 015 (C), one 50g ball in Lime 025 (D), two 50g balls in Dark Olive Green 024 (E) and Pale Blue 026 (F) and 2 (3, 3, 3) 50g balls in Ecru 101 (G).
● Pair each of 3mm (US 2) and 3.25mm (US 3) knitting needles.
● 9 buttons.

TENSION
■ 27 sts and 34 rows to 10cm/4in square over Fair Isle st st using 3.25mm (US 3) needles.

BACK
With 3mm (US 2) needles and E, cast on 129 (145, 161, 177) sts.
Beg with a k row, work 3 rows in st st.
Picot row (wrong side) P1, [yrn, p2tog] to end.
Change to 3.25mm (US 3) needles and F.
Beg with a k row, work 2 rows in st st.
Change to M.
Beg with a k row, work in st st and patt from Chart 1.
Work 6 (6, 8, 8) rows.
Dec one st at each end of the next row and every foll 6th row until there are 117 (133, 149, 165) sts, at the same time, when all 20 rows of chart 1 have been worked, work repeats of 40 rows of chart 2 only.
Work 11 (11, 13, 13) rows.
Inc one st at each end of the next row and every foll 10th row until there are 127 (143, 159, 175) sts.
Work straight until back measures 30 (30, 31, 31) cm/12 (12, 12¼, 12¼)in from picot row, ending with a wrong side row.
Shape armholes
Cast off 8 (9, 10, 11) sts at beg of next 2 rows.
111 (125, 139, 153) sts.
Dec one st at each end of the next 5 (7, 11, 13) rows, then every foll right side row until 89 (97, 105, 113) sts rem.
Work straight until back measures 50 (51, 53, 54)cm/19¾ (20, 21, 21¼)in from picot row, ending with a wrong side row.
Shape shoulders
Cast off 12 (14, 15, 16) sts at beg of next 2 rows and 12 (13, 14, 16) sts on foll 2 rows.
Leave the rem 41 (43, 47, 49) sts on a holder.

LEFT FRONT
With 3mm (US 2) needles and E, cast on 65 (73, 81, 89) sts.
Beg with a k row, work 3 rows in st st.
Picot row (wrong side) P1, [yrn, p2tog] to end.
Change to 3.25mm (US 3) needles and F.

notes
✳ Read charts from right to left on right side rows and from left to right on wrong side rows. When working in pattern, strand yarn not in use loosely across wrong side of work to keep fabric elastic.

abbreviations
yf = yarn forward and over needle to make one st.
yrn = yarn round needle to make one st.
Also see page 123.

Fair Isle Cardigan

Beg with a k row, work 2 rows in st st.

Change to M.

Beg with a k row, work in st st and patt from Chart 1.

Work 6 (6, 8, 8) rows.

Dec one st at beg of next row and every foll 6th row until there are 59 (67, 75, 83) sts, at the same time, when all 20 rows of chart 1 have been worked, work repeats of 40 rows of chart 2 only.

Work 11 (11, 13, 13) rows.

Inc one st at beg of the next row and every foll 10th row until there are 64 (72, 80, 88) sts.

Work straight until front measures 30 (30, 31, 31)cm/12 (12, 12¼, 12¼)in from picot row, ending with a wrong side row.

Shape armhole

Cast off 8 (9, 10, 11) sts at beg of next row. 56 (63, 70, 77) sts.

Work 1 row.

Dec one st at armhole edge of the next 5 (7, 11, 13) rows, then every foll right side row until 45 (49, 53, 57) sts rem.

Work straight until front measures 42 (43, 45, 46)cm/16½ (17, 17¾, 18)in from picot row, ending with a wrong side row.

Shape neck

Next row (right side) Patt to last 10 (11, 11, 12) sts, turn, leaving rem sts on a holder for neck edging.

Dec one st at neck edge on every row until 24 (27, 29, 32) sts rem.

Work straight until front measures same as Back to shoulder, ending at armhole edge.

Shape shoulder

Cast off 12 (14, 15, 16) sts at beg of next row.

Work 1 row.

Cast off rem 12 (13, 14, 16) sts.

RIGHT FRONT

With 3mm (US 2) needles and E, cast on 65 (73, 81, 89) sts.

Beg with a k row, work 3 rows in st st.

Picot row (wrong side) P1, [yrn, p2tog] to end.

Change to 3.25mm (US 3) needles and F.

Beg with a k row, work 2 rows in st st.

Change to M.

Beg with a k row, work in st st and patt from Chart 1.

Chart 1

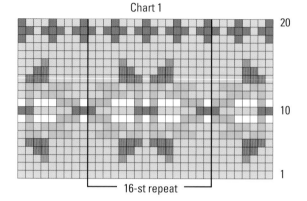

16-st repeat

Chart 2

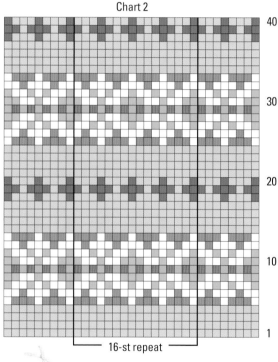

16-st repeat

Color Key

☐ Silver (MC, 012)	☐ Lime (D)
☐ Mid blue (A)	■ Forest Green (E)
■ Red (B, 700)	☐ Pale Blue (F)
☐ Pink (C, 015)	☐ Ecru (G,101)

Fair Isle Cardigan

Back & Fronts

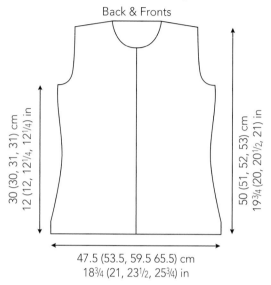

30 (30, 31, 31) cm
12 (12, 12¼, 12¼) in

50 (51, 52, 53) cm
19¾ (20, 20½, 21) in

47.5 (53.5, 59.5 65.5) cm
18¾ (21, 23½, 25¾) in

Sleeves

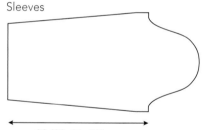

30 (30, 31, 31) cm
12 (12, 12¼, 12¼) in

Work 6 (6, 8, 8) rows.

Dec one st at beg of next row and every foll 6th row until there are 59 (67, 75, 83) sts, AT THE SAME TIME, when all 20 rows of chart 1 have been worked, work repeats of 40 rows of chart 2 only.

Work 11 (11, 13, 13) rows.

Inc one st at beg of the next and every foll 10th row until there are 64 (72, 80, 88) sts.

Work straight until front measures 30 (30, 31, 31)cm/12 (12, 12¼, 12¼)in from picot row, ending with a right side row.

Shape armhole

Cast off 8 (9, 10, 11) sts at beg of next row. 56 (63, 70, 77) sts.

Dec one st at armhole edge of the next 5 (7, 11, 13) rows, then every foll right side row until 45 (49, 53, 57) sts rem.

Work straight until front measures 42 (43, 45, 46)cm/16½ (17, 17¾, 18) in from picot row, ending with a wrong side row.

Shape neck

Next row Patt 10 (11, 11, 12) sts, leave these sts on a holder, patt to end.

Dec one st at neck edge on every row until 24 (27, 29, 32) sts rem. Work straight until front measures same as Back to shoulder, ending at armhole edge.

Shape shoulder

Cast off 12 (14, 15, 16) sts at beg of next row.

Work 1 row.

Cast off rem 12 (13, 14, 16) sts.

SLEEVES

With 3mm (US 2) needles and E, cast on 65 (71, 77, 83) sts.

Beg with a k row, work 3 rows in st st.

Picot row (wrong side) P1, [yrn, p2tog] to end.

Change to 3.25mm (US 3) needles and D.

Beg with a k row, work 2 rows in st st.

Change to M.

Beg with a k row, work in st st and patt from Chart 1.

Work 4 rows.

Inc one st at each end of the next row and every foll 6th row until there are 95 (101, 107, 113) sts, AT THE SAME TIME, when all 20 rows of chart 1 have been worked, work repeats of 40 rows of chart 2 only, taking all inc sts into patt.

Work straight until sleeve measures 30 (30, 31, 31)cm/12 (12, 12¼, 12¼)in from picot row, ending with a wrong side row.

Shape top

Cast off 8 (9, 10, 11) sts at beg of next 2 rows. 79 (83, 87, 91) sts.

Dec one st at each end of the next 5 rows, then 3 (5, 7, 9) foll right side rows, now dec one st at each end of every foll 4th row until 57 sts rem.

Dec one st at each end of next row and 4 foll right side rows, then at each end of next 5 rows. 37 sts.

Cast off 6 sts at beg of next 4 rows.

Cast off rem 13 sts.

NECKBAND

Join shoulder seams.

With right side facing, 3.25mm (US 3) needles and M, slip 10 (11, 11, 12) sts from right front neck holder onto a needle, pick up and k29 sts up right front neck, k across 41 (43, 47, 49) sts from back neck holder, pick up and k29 sts down left front neck, then k10 (11, 11, 12) sts from left front holder. 119 (123, 127, 131) sts.

Change to C.

Beg with a p row, work 2 rows in st st.

Change to E.

P 1 row.

Picot row (right side) K1, [yf, k2tog] to end.

Change to 3mm (US 2) needles.

Work 3 rows in st st.

Cast off.

BUTTON BAND

With right side facing, 3mm (US 2) needles and M, pick up and k96 (100, 104, 108) sts along left front edge between picot rows.

K 3 rows.

Cast off.

BUTTONHOLE BAND

With right side facing, 3mm (US 2) needles and M, pick up and k96 (98, 106, 108) sts along right front edge between picot rows.

K 1 row.

Buttonhole row (right side) K3 (4, 4, 5), yrn, k2tog, [k9 (9, 10, 10), yrn, k2tog] 8 times, k3 (4, 4, 5).

K 1 row.

Cast off.

TO MAKE UP

Join side and sleeve seams. Sew sleeves into armholes easing to fit. Fold hems onto wrong side along picot row and slipstitch in position. Sew on buttons. ❖

Tweed Jacket with Contrast Lining

A flash of unexpected color gives a classic tweed jacket a contemporary twist.

TO FIT BUST
81, 86, 92, 97, 102, 107 cm
32, 34, 36, 38, 40, 42 in

FINISHED MEASUREMENTS
BUST
90, 94, 99, 103, 107, 112 cm
35½, 37, 39, 40½, 42, 44 in

LENGTH TO SHOULDER
60, 61, 62, 63, 64, 65 cm
23½, 24, 24½, 24¾, 25½, 25¾ in

SLEEVE LENGTH
44, 44, 45, 45, 46, 46 cm
17¼, 17¼, 17¾, 17¾, 18, 18 in

MATERIALS
● 11 (12, 13, 14, 15, 16) 50g balls of Debbie Bliss Donegal Luxury Tweed in Burgundy 16 (M) and 1 (1, 2, 2, 2, 2) 50g balls of Debbie Bliss Rialto Aran in Fuchsia 14 (C).
● Pair each 4.50mm (US 7) and 5mm (US 8) knitting needles.
● 8 buttons.

TENSION
■ 18 sts and 29 rows to 10cm/4in square over moss st with M, using 5mm (US 8) needles.

BACK
With 5mm (US 8) needles and M, cast on 89 (93, 97, 101, 105, 109) sts.
Moss st row K1, [p1, k1] to end.
Rep the last row 11 times more.
13th row Moss st 15 (16, 17, 18, 19, 20), work 3tog, moss st to last 18 (19, 20, 21, 22, 23) sts, work 3tog, moss st 15 (16, 17, 18, 19, 20).
Work 9 rows.
23rd row Moss st 14 (15, 16, 17, 18, 19), work 3tog, moss st to last 17 (18, 19, 20, 21, 22) sts, work 3tog, moss st 14 (15, 16, 17, 18, 19).
Work 9 rows.
33rd row Moss st 13 (14, 15, 16, 17, 18), work 3tog, moss st to last 16 (17, 18, 19, 20, 21) sts, work 3tog, moss st 13 (14, 15, 16, 17, 18).
Work 9 rows.
43rd row Moss st 12 (13, 14, 15, 16, 17), work 3tog, moss st to last 15 (16, 17, 18, 19, 20) sts, work 3tog, moss st 12 (13, 14, 15, 16, 17).
Work 9 rows.
53rd row Moss st 11 (12, 13, 14, 15, 16), work 3tog, moss st to last 14 (15, 16, 17, 18, 19) sts, work 3tog, moss st 11 (12, 13, 14, 15, 16). 69 (73, 77, 81, 85, 89) sts.
Cont straight until back measures 24cm/9½in from cast on edge, ending with a wrong side row.
Next row Moss st 11 (12, 13, 14, 15, 16), m1, moss st 1, m1, moss st to last 12 (13, 14, 15, 16, 17) sts, m1, moss st 1, m1, moss st 11 (12, 13, 14, 15, 16).
Work 15 rows.
Next row Moss st 12 (13, 14, 15, 16, 17), m1, moss st 1, m1, moss st to last 13 (14, 15, 16, 17, 18) sts, m1, moss st 1, m1, moss st 12 (13, 14, 15, 16, 17).
Work 15 rows.
Next row Moss st 13(14, 15, 16, 17, 18), m1, moss st 1, m1, moss st to last 14 (15, 16, 17, 18, 19) sts, m1, moss st 1, m1, moss st 13 (14, 15, 16, 17, 18). 81 (85, 89, 93, 97, 101) sts.
Cont straight until back measures 40cm/15¾in from cast on edge, ending with a wrong side row.

abbreviations

y2rn = yarn round needle twice, working p1, k1 into y2rn on following row.
See page 123.

Tweed Jacket with Contrast Lining

Shape armholes

Cast off 6 sts at beg of next 2 rows. 69 (73, 77, 81, 85, 89) sts.

Dec one st at each end of next row and every foll right side row until 61 (63, 65, 67, 69, 71) sts rem.

Cont in moss st until back measures 60 (61, 62, 63, 64, 65)cm/23½ (24, 24½, 24¾, 25½, 25¾)in from cast on edge, ending with a wrong side row.

Shape shoulders

Cast off 9 (9, 9, 10, 10, 10) sts at beg of next 2 rows and 9 (10, 10, 10, 10, 11) sts at beg of foll 2 rows.

Cast off rem 25 (25, 27, 27, 29, 29) sts.

POCKET LININGS (make 2)

With 5mm (US 8) needles and C, cast on 22 (22, 22, 24, 24, 24) sts.

Beg with a k row, work 45 rows in st st.

Leave these sts on a holder.

LEFT FRONT

With 5mm (US 8) needles and M, cast on 47 (49, 51, 53, 55, 57) sts.

Moss st row P1, [k1, p1] to end.

Rep the last row 11 times more.

13th row Moss st 15 (16, 17, 18, 19, 20), work 3tog, moss st to end.

Work 9 rows.

23rd row Moss st 14 (15, 16, 17, 18, 19), work 3tog, moss st to end.

Work 9 rows.

33rd row Moss st 13 (14, 15, 16, 17, 18), work 3tog, moss st to end.

Work 9 rows.

43rd row Moss st 12 (13, 14, 15, 16, 17), work 3tog, moss st to end.

Work 9 rows.

53rd row Moss st 11 (12, 13, 14, 15, 16), work 3tog, moss st to end. 37 (39, 41, 43, 45, 47) sts

Work 1 row.

Place pocket

Next row Moss st 6 (7, 8, 8, 9, 10), cast off next 22 (22, 22, 24, 24, 24) sts, moss st to end.

Next row Moss st 9 (10, 11, 11, 12, 13), p across sts of pocket lining, moss st to end.

Cont straight in moss st until front measures 24cm/9½ in from cast on edge, ending with a wrong side row.

Next row Moss st 11 (12, 13, 14, 15, 16), m1, moss st 1, m1, moss st to end.

Work 15 rows.

Next row Moss st 12 (13, 14, 15, 16, 17), m1, moss st 1, m1, moss st to end.

Work 15 rows.

Next row Moss st 13 (14, 15, 16, 17, 18), m1, moss st 1, m1, moss st to end. 43 (45, 47, 49, 51, 53) sts.

Cont straight until front measures 40cm/15¾ in from cast on edge, ending with a wrong side row.

Shape armhole

Cast off 6 sts at beg of next row. 37 (39, 41, 43, 45, 47) sts.

Work 1 row.

Dec one st at armhole edge of next row and every foll right side row until 33 (34, 35, 36, 37, 38) sts rem.

Work straight until front measures 54 (55, 55, 56, 56, 57)cm/21¼ (21¾, 21¾, 22, 22, 22½)in from cast on edge, ending with a wrong side row.

Shape neck

Next row Moss st to last 10 (10, 11, 11, 12, 12) sts, turn and leave these sts on a holder.

Dec one st at neck edge of next row and every foll alt row until 18 (19, 19, 20, 20, 21) sts rem.

Cont straight until front matches Back to shoulder shaping, ending at armhole edge.

Shape shoulder

Cast off 9 (9, 9, 10, 10, 10) sts at beg of next row.

Work 1 row.

Cast off rem 9 (10, 10, 10, 10, 11) sts.

RIGHT FRONT

Mark position for 7 buttons, the first 4cm/1½in from lower edge, the seventh 2cm/¾in from neck edge and the rem 5 spaced evenly between.

Work buttonhole to match markers as follows:

Buttonhole row (right side) P1, k1, p1, k2tog, y2rn, p2tog,

Tweed Jacket with Contrast Lining

moss st to end.

With 5mm (US 8) needles and M, cast on 47 (49, 51, 53, 55, 57) sts.

Moss st row P1, [k1, p1] to end.

Rep the last row 11 times more.

13th row Moss st to last 18 (19, 20, 21, 22, 23) sts, work 3tog, moss st 15 (16, 17, 18, 19, 20).

Work 9 rows.

23rd row Moss st to last 17 (18, 19, 20, 21, 22) sts, work 3tog, moss st 14 (15, 16, 17, 18, 19).

Work 9 rows.

33rd row Moss st to last 16 (17, 18, 19, 20, 21) sts, work 3tog, moss st 13 (14, 15, 16, 17, 18).

Work 9 rows.

43rd row Moss st to last 15 (16, 17, 18, 19, 20) sts, work 3tog, moss st 12 (13, 14, 15, 16, 17).

Work 9 rows.

53rd row Moss st to last 14 (15, 16, 17, 18, 19) sts, work 3tog, moss st 11 (12, 13, 14, 15, 16). 37 (39, 41, 43, 45, 47) sts

Work 1 row.

Place pocket

Next row Moss st 9 (10, 11, 11, 12, 13), cast off next 22 (22, 22, 24, 24, 24) sts, moss st to end.

Next row Moss st 6 (7, 8, 8, 9, 10), p across sts of pocket lining, moss st to end.

Cont straight in moss st until front measures 24cm/9½in from cast on edge, ending with a wrong side row.

Next row Moss st to last 12 (13, 14, 15, 16, 17) sts, m1, moss st 1, m1, moss st 11 (12, 13, 14, 15, 16).

Work 15 rows.

Next row Moss st to last 13 (14, 15, 16, 17, 18) sts, m1, moss st 1, m1, moss st 12 (13, 14, 15, 16, 17).

Work 15 rows.

Next row Moss st to last 14 (15, 16, 17, 18, 19) sts, m1, moss st 1, m1, moss st 13 (14, 15, 16, 17, 18). 43 (45, 47, 49, 51, 53) sts.

Cont straight until front measures 40cm/15¾in from cast on edge, ending with a right side row.

Shape armhole

Cast off 6 sts at beg of next row. 37 (39, 41, 43, 45, 47) sts.

Dec one st at armhole edge of next row and every foll right side row until 33 (34, 35, 36, 37, 38) sts rem.

Work straight until front measures 54 (55, 55, 56, 56, 57)cm/21¼ (21¾, 21¾, 22, 22, 22½)in from cast on edge, ending with a wrong side row.

Shape neck

Next row Moss st 10 (10, 11, 11, 12, 12) sts, leave these sts on a holder, moss st to end.

Dec one st at neck edge of next row and every foll alt row until 18 (19, 19, 20, 20, 21) sts rem.

Cont straight until front matches Back to shoulder shaping, ending at armhole edge.

Shape shoulder

Cast off 9 (9, 9, 10, 10, 10) sts at beg of next row.

Work 1 row.

Cast off rem 9 (10, 10, 10, 10, 11) sts.

SLEEVES

Cuff - 1st half

With 5mm (US 8) needles and M, cast on 18 (19, 20, 21, 22, 23) sts

1st row K1, [p1, k1] to last 1 (0, 1, 0, 1, 0) sts, p1 (0, 1, 0, 1, 0).

2nd row P1 (0, 1, 0, 1, 0), k1, [p1, k1] to end.

Rep the last 2 rows 5 times more.

Break off yarn and leave these sts on a holder.

Cuff - 2nd half

With 5mm (US 8) needles and M, cast on 18 (19, 20, 21, 22, 23) sts

1st row P1 (0, 1, 0, 1, 0), k1, [p1, k1] to end.

2nd row K1, [p1, k1] to last 1 (0, 1, 0, 1, 0) sts, p1 (0, 1, 0, 1, 0).

Rep the last 2 rows 5 times more.

Next row Moss st 17 (18, 19, 20, 21, 22), k last st tog with first st of first half of cuff, moss st 17 (18, 19, 20, 21, 22). 35 (37, 39, 41, 43, 45) sts.

Work 7 rows in moss st.

Place markers at each end of last row.

Change to C and 4.50mm (US 7) needles.

Next row (right side) K to end.

Beg with a k row, work 9 rows in reverse st st.

Change to M.

Next row (right side) K to end.

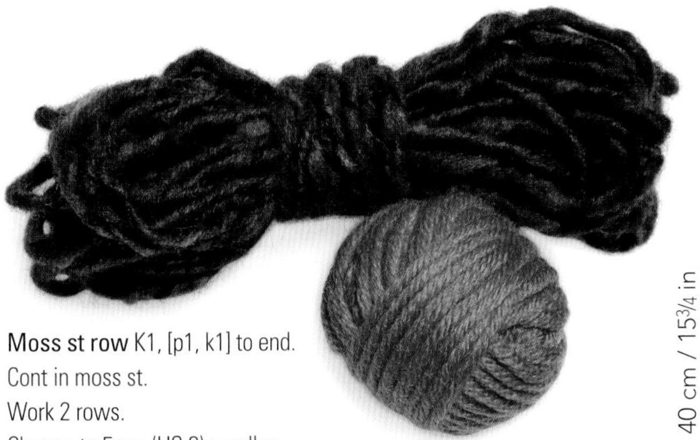

Moss st row K1, [p1, k1] to end.
Cont in moss st.
Work 2 rows.
Change to 5mm (US 8) needles.
Inc one st at each end of the next row and every foll 10th (10th, 8th, 8th, 8th, 8th) row until there are 55 (59, 63, 67, 71, 73) sts.
Cont straight until sleeve measures 44 (44, 45, 45, 46, 46)cm/17¼ (17¼, 17¾, 17¾, 18, 18)in from markers, ending with a wrong side row.

Shape sleeve top
Cast off 6 sts st beg of next 2 rows. 43 (47, 51, 55, 59, 61) sts.
Dec 1 st at each end of the next row and every foll 4th row until 31 (33, 35, 37, 39, 39) sts rem, then on every foll right side row until 19 (21, 23, 25, 27, 29) sts rem.
Work 1 row.
Cast off 3 sts at beg of next 2 rows.
Cast off rem 13 (15, 17, 19, 21, 23) sts.

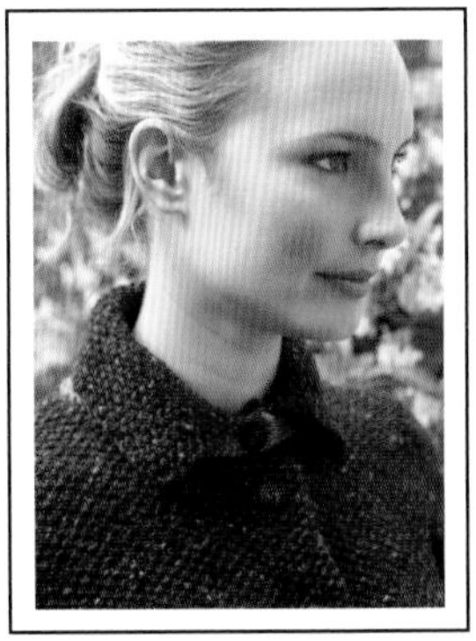

COLLAR
Join shoulder seams.
With 4.50mm (US 7) needles and M, slip 10 (10, 11, 11, 12, 12) sts from right front holder onto a needle, pick up and k14 (14, 16, 16, 18, 18) sts up right front to shoulder, 25 (25, 27, 27, 29, 29) sts from back neck, 14 (14, 16, 16, 18, 18) sts down left front, then moss st 10 (10, 11, 11, 12, 12) sts from left front holder. 73 (73, 81, 81, 89, 89) sts.
Next row K to end.
Change to C.
K 4 rows.
Buttonhole row K2, k2tog, y2rn, skpo, k to end.
Next row K, working into front and back of y2rn.
K 2 rows.
Change to M.

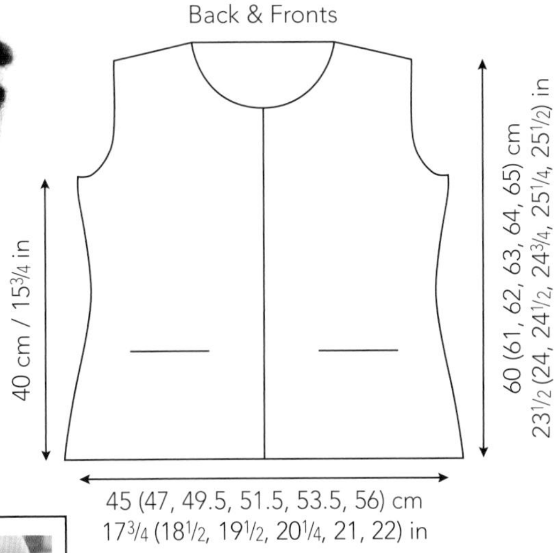
Back & Fronts
40 cm / 15¾ in
60 (61, 62, 63, 64, 65) cm
23½ (24, 24½, 24¾, 25¼, 25½) in
45 (47, 49.5, 51.5, 53.5, 56) cm
17¾ (18½, 19½, 20¼, 21, 22) in

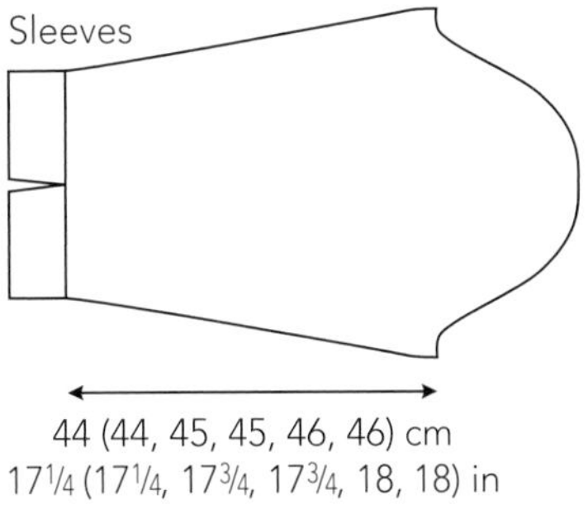
Sleeves
44 (44, 45, 45, 46, 46) cm
17¼ (17¼, 17¾, 17¾, 18, 18) in

Next row K to end.
Cont in moss st.
Next 2 rows Work to last 25 sts, turn.
Next 2 rows Work to last 20 sts, turn.
Next 2 rows Work to last 15 sts, turn.
Next 2 rows Work to last 10 sts, turn.
Next 2 rows Work to last 5 sts, turn.
Next row Moss st to end.
Cast off 3 sts at beg of next 2 rows.
Change to 5mm (US 8) needles.
Cont in moss st for a further 8cm/3in.
Cast off in moss st.

TO MAKE UP
Join shoulder seams. Join side and sleeve seams. Sew sleeves into armholes, easing to fit. Sew down pocket linings. Sew on buttons. Fold cuffs up onto right side. ❇

3 designing with texture

designing with texture

I have a great passion for texture—I love the way that by simply combining knit and purl stitches you can create a three-dimensional landscape of knitted fabric. Looking at a blanket or afghan made from a creative combination of stitch patterns can have a similar effect on me as looking at a great painting. Working the swatches as I start on a design allows me to take the journey that makes designing hand knits forever fascinating. I am rarely happy with the first swatch, it's usually just a starting point and other ideas evolve from it.

Swatch A is an example of one such journey. Working on a child's design, I knitted up a simple diamond cable with a garter stitch center that I'd imagined would be perfect for a tunic. But looking at the finished swatch, I felt that the space between the diamonds created a "blank canvas" of fabric that looked uninteresting and unattractive. When I introduced a panel of garter stitch with bobbles, the fabric seemed to come alive. In order to link the texture, I made the borders in garter stitch with a picot edge that echoed the shape of the bobbles, as you can see in swatch B.

That design led to another one (swatch C). This time I put the diamond cables together in panels and introduced bobbles into the spaces of reverse stockinette between them. These bobbles then ran down into a welt of rib and cables, where the four-stitch cable echoed the cables of the main pattern.

The principle of "echoing" is something that I use a lot in my work. It's where I take an integral part of a design—the shape of a cable or the stitch within it—and use it elsewhere. The effect is one of harmony throughout the whole design. Maybe the borders or hems are in seed stitch instead of the usual rib, the cables run down into the ribs, or a border is built of garter stitch triangles to work with the diamond cable.

When working on Aran-style garments, I play around with different panels of patterns until I find a sequence that's satisfying. In swatch D, the center panel is made up of stitches that are worked into the back, giving a defining linear look to them. The accompanying panels on either side and the welt also use this style of stitchwork. The side panels were chosen to balance the trellis effect of the center panel. Balance is essential, whether in the proportions of a style or in the careful choosing of a four-stitch over a six-stitch cable. Too-small cables can look skinny and disappear into the background, but a too-large one might overpower the other textures.

If you want to create your own Aran design, start by looking for cable stitch patterns that have a similar feel. Knit up single pattern panels and arrange them side-by-side until you feel you have the most satisfying sequence. Trust your eye: You will easily see what works and what doesn't. Think about what smaller cables you may want to run between the larger ones for additional balance, and think about the selvedges, looking for a stitch within a cable that would work at each side of the pieces.

Then think about how to "frame" the design with the hem and cuffs; the borders of the design are as important as the work within it. I compare it to choosing a frame for a picture that you love—the frame should relate to the work, not overpower it or

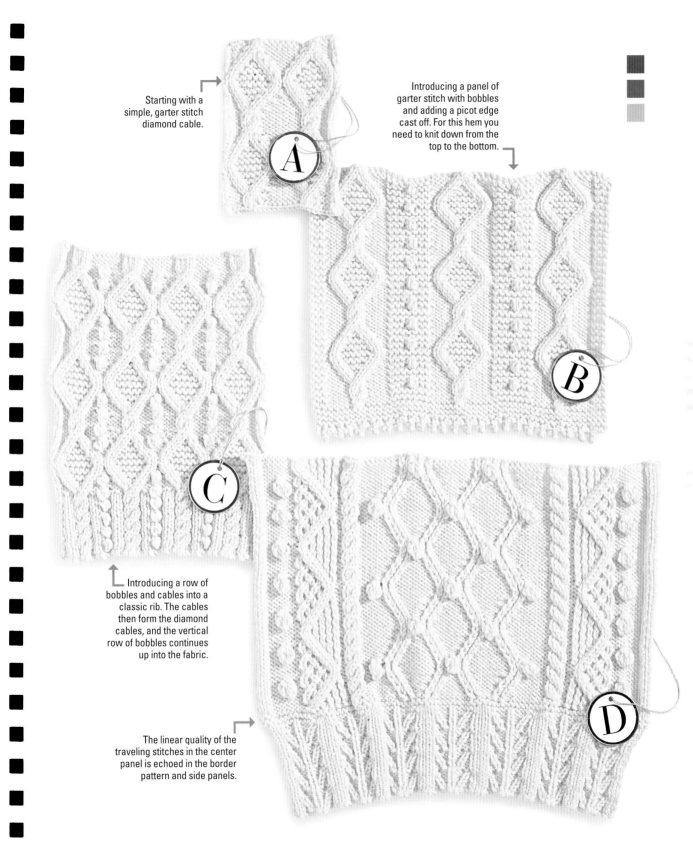

Starting with a simple, garter stitch diamond cable.

A

Introducing a panel of garter stitch with bobbles and adding a picot edge cast off. For this hem you need to knit down from the top to the bottom.

B

C

Introducing a row of bobbles and cables into a classic rib. The cables then form the diamond cables, and the vertical row of bobbles continues up into the fabric.

The linear quality of the traveling stitches in the center panel is echoed in the border pattern and side panels.

D

designing with texture

look inappropriate. I find that a simple rib rarely works, because it can pull in too much, but seed stitch, which isn't as elastic, can create a sense of balance. Work up swatches to see what looks good in your own designs.

When working on your first multi-textured design it is better to choose a very basic shape, with a minimum of armhole shaping. This is because you don't want the shaping to interrupt too many of the stitch patterns on the body, which will not only look unattractive but also make the stitch panel very difficult to follow. For this reason it is better to have a simple pattern at the side edges, such as seed stitch or panels of small cables. Dropped shoulders, in which there is no armole shaping, of course, fits the bill perfectly, but, when knitted in a thicker yarn, can lead to too much bulky fabric underneath the arm. A better solution is to work a square, set-in sleeve where some stitches are initially cast off, then work the body straight. Increasing into patterns—especially on sleeves—can be problematic. Therefore, I would choose a main pattern that is on the body, run it up the center of the sleeve with the simpler patterns, such as stockinette stitch, at the side, thus working the shaping into the easier pattern.

When you know the width that you want your garment, arrange the pattern panels that you have worked in the sequence you have decided on, choosing one to be used centrally. To get the right measurement you will need only half of the panels required to make the whole width, as you can double the amount of stitches required so your pattern will be symmetrical. If you need more stitches to achieve the desired width, add more pattern panels or more selvedge stitches, and if you need fewer, take stitches away. There should be no need to knit a swatch across all the stitches for the front and back of your garment, but you should add some extra stitches to allow for the fabric to come in when worked over a larger number of stitches, particularly if worked in an elastic yarn such as wool, which will pull in more. To make your design look as professional as possible make sure that your cable crosses are not too near your central cast-off stitches for your neck shaping, as this will make the neckband lie less flat. On the shoulders, try to end on a whole or half a pattern so that when the shoulder pieces are sewn up, the pattern is complete.

Finally, choose your yarn carefully! You will need one that gives great stitch definition. Wool and wool blends give a good, even surface as the elasticity of the yarn will make the fibers close up when the stitches are pulled away in cables. Cotton will give crispness to the stitches and show them off beautifully, but it's not as elastic as wool, and there can sometimes be a slight ladder where the cable stitches are twisted. Despite this drawback, a classic cotton Aran can be a perfect summer cover-up. ▨

Top Texture Tips

▶ Keep a simple shape when designing your first Aran pattern; with a heavily textured pattern you will need to keep armhole shaping to a minimum, or use a dropped shoulder.

▶ Think about carrying patterns such as cables into ribbed bands (see Multi-Texture Throw, on page 68).

▶ Use a yarn that gives great stitch definition.

patterns

These three designs demonstrate my approach to texture.

Herringbone & Cable Jacket

Worked in extra-fine merino in an Aran weight, this jacket features a simple dropped-shoulder shape, which means that armhole shaping doesn't interfere with the stitch pattern. The easy shaping also gives a casual, weekend feel. I love blackberry or astrakhan stitch, but it is notoriously difficult to work shaping in, so I made sure that the panels were within the main body. A basic collar, knit from the body in one reversible piece, tops it off. Working a collar in this way, rather than picking up stitches and folding it back, doesn't produce an ugly seam which would be undesirable. To add interest to an otherwise simple design, a large cable pattern runs up the back and into the collar.

Multi-Texture Throw

There is double moss stitch, garter stitch, a cable and a lace pattern in this throw. The cables run down into the ribs at the top and bottom and, in order to keep the side edging from pulling in and to create an attractive effect, the sides are worked in garter stitch. The vertical patterns are all separated by a cable, but because each pattern behaves differently, with the cables drawing the fabric in and the garter stitch expanding it, there is a wavy feel. Each pattern was carefully placed to balance the others out, so the final effect is controlled, making this throw both attractive and warm. The Cashmerino-mix yarn makes it beautifully soft—the perfect throw for a cool evening or to wrap a baby in.

Bobble & Cable Sweater

I wanted to take all the classic elements of a traditional Aran sweater and create a prettier, more delicate design. I started off with the main, intricate central cable panel and introduced bobbles there. I then picked a simpler cable with bobbles and a bigger woven cable and divided them up with a small four-stitch cable. Rather than go with a classic rib edging, I took the rib elements, cabled them, added bobbles to tie in with the bobbles on the body, and finished off with a delicate picot edge. I made the neck wider to create a more feminine feel. By slightly shaping the body in at the sides, a casual, classic aran is given a smarter, more modern feel.

Herringbone & Cable Jacket

A casual, hip-length jacket with a relaxed fold-over collar. The combination of herringbone and blackberry stitch contrasts with the dramatic cable on the back.

TO FIT BUST
81–86, 92–97 cm
32-34, 36–38 in

FINISHED MEASUREMENTS
WIDTH ACROSS BACK
44, 50 cm
17¼, 19¾ in

LENGTH TO SHOULDER
51, 56 cm
20, 22 in

Sleeve length
45, 46 cm
17¾, 18 in

MATERIALS
● 17(19) 50g balls of Debbie Bliss Rialto Aran in Duck Egg 23.
● Pair each 4.50mm (US 7) and 5mm (US 8) knitting needles.
● 4.50mm (US 7) circular needle.
● Cable needle.

TENSION
■ 21 sts and 32 rows to 10cm/4in square over herringbone patt using 5mm (US 8) needles.

PATTERN PANEL
Worked over 49 sts.
1st row (right side) [P2, k4] 4 times, p1, [k4, p2] 4 times.
2nd, 4th, 6th, 8th and 10th rows [K2, p4] 4 times, k1, [p4, k2] 4 times.
3rd row [P2, C4F, p2, k4] twice, p1, [k4, p2, C4B, p2] twice.
5th row As 1st row.
7th row P2, C4F, p2, k4, p2, C4F, p2, Cr9F, p2, C4B, p2, k4, p2, C4B, p2.
9th row As 1st row.
11th row P2, C4F, p2, k4, p2, C4F, Cr6R, p1, Cr6L, C4B, p2, k4, p2, C4B, p2.
12th row K2, [p4, k2] twice, p10, k1, p10, [k2, p4] twice, k2.
13th row P2, k4, p2, Cr5LP, p1, k2, Cr6RP, k2, p1, k2, Cr6LP, k2, p1, Cr5RP, p2, k4, p2.
14th row K2, p4, k3, p4, k1, p6, k2, p2, k1, p2, k2, p6, k1, p4, k3, p4, k2.
15th row P2, C4F, p3, Cr5LP, Cr6RP, p2, k2, p1, k2, p2, Cr6LP, Cr5RP, p3, C4B, p2.
16th row K2, p4, k4, p8, k4, p2, k1, p2, k4, p8, k4, p4, k2.
17th row P2, k4, p4, C8F, p4, Cr5F, p4, C8B, p4, k4, p2.
18th row As 16th row.
19th row P2, C4F, p3, Cr5RP, Cr6L, p2, k2, p1, k2, p2, Cr6R, Cr5LP, p3, C4B, p2.
20th row As 14th row.
21st row P2, k4, p2, Cr5RP, p1, k2, Cr6L, k2, p1, k2, Cr6R, k2, p1, Cr5LP, p2, k4, p2.
22nd row As 12th row.
23rd row P2, C4F, p2, k4, p2, C4F, Cr6LP, p1, Cr6RP, C4B, p2, k4, p2, C4B, p2.
24th and 26th rows As 2nd row.
25th row As 1st row.

abbreviations

C4B = sl 2 sts onto cable needle and hold at back of work, k2, then k2 from cable needle.

C4F = sl 2 sts onto cable needle and hold to front of work, k2, then k2 from cable needle.

Cr5F = sl 3 sts onto cable needle and hold to front of work, k2, sl p st back onto left needle and p it, then k rem 2 sts from cable needle.

Cr5LP = sl 4 sts onto cable needle and hold to front of work, p1, then k4 from cable needle.

Cr5RP = sl 1 st onto cable needle and hold at back of work, k4, then p1 from cable needle.

Cr6L = sl 4 sts onto cable needle and hold to front of work, k2, then k4 from cable needle.

Cr6LP = sl 4 sts onto cable needle and hold to front

of work, p2, then k4 from cable needle.

Cr6R = sl 2 sts onto cable needle and hold at back of work, k4, then k2 from cable needle.

Cr6RP = sl 2 sts onto cable needle and hold at back of work, k4, then p2 from cable needle.

C8B = sl next 4 sts onto cable needle and hold at back of work, k4, then k4 from cable needle.

C8F = sl 4 sts onto cable needle and hold to front of work, k4, then k4 from cable needle.

Cr9F = sl 5 sts onto cable needle and hold to front of work, k4, slip p st back onto left needle and p it, then k rem 4 sts from cable needle.

kpk = [k1, p1, k1] into next st.

Also see page 123.

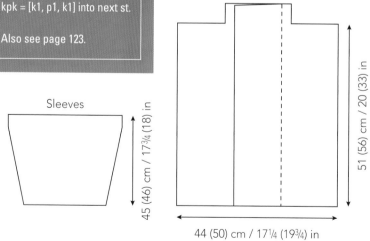

Back & Fronts

51 (56) cm / 20 (33) in

44 (50) cm / 17¼ (19¾) in

Sleeves

45 (46) cm / 17¾ (18) in

Herringbone & Cable Jacket

27th row As 7th row.
28th row As 2nd row.
These 28 rows form the pattern panel and are repeated.

BACK
With 4.50mm (US 7) needles, cast on 109(121) sts.
Moss st row K1, [p1, k1] to end.
This row forms moss st.
Work a further 4 rows in moss st.
Inc row Moss st 35 (41), m1, moss st 12, m1, moss st 15, m1, moss st 12, m1, moss st to end. 113 (125) sts.
Change to 5mm (US 8) needles.
1st row (right side) [P1, k2, p2, k3, p2, k2] 2 (3) times, p1, k2 (0), p2 (0), k3 (1), work across 1st row of patt panel, k3 (1), p2 (0), k2 (0), p1, [k2, p2, k3, p2, k2, p1] 2 (3) times.
2nd row [K2, p2, k2, p1, k2, p2, k1] 2 (3) times, k2 (1), p2 (1), k2 (0), p2 (0), work across 2nd row of patt panel, p2 (1), k2 (1), p2 (0), k2 (0), [k1, p2, k2, p1, k2, p2, k2] 2 (3) times.
3rd row [K1, p2, k2, p3, k2, p2] 2 (3) times, k1, p2 (0), k2 (0), p2 (0), k1, work across 3rd row of patt panel, k1, p2 (0), k2 (0), p2 (0), k1, [p2, k2, p3, k2, p2, k1] 2 (3) times.
4th row [P2, k2, p2, k1, p2, k2, p1] 2 (3) times, p2, k2 (0), p2 (0), k1 (0), p1 (0), work across 4th row of patt panel , p1 (2), k1 (0), p2 (0), k2 (0), p2 (0), [p1, k2, p2, k1, p2, k2, p2] 2 (3) times.
These 4 rows form the herringbone patt and set the position of the patt panel and are repeated, working correct patt panel rows until back measures 51 (56)cm/20 (22)in from cast on edge, ending with a 4th row.
Shape shoulders
Cast off 27 (33) sts at beg of next 2 rows.
Leave rem 59 sts on a holder.

LEFT FRONT
With 4.50mm (US 7) needles, cast on 78 (84) sts.
1st moss st row (right side) [P1, k1] to end.
2nd moss st row [K1, p1] to end.
Rep these 2 rows once more then the 1st row again.
Inc row [Moss st 22, m1] twice, moss st 34 (40). 80(86) sts.

Change to 5mm (US 8) needles.
1st row (right side) [P1, k2, p2, k3, p2, k2] 2 (3) times, p1, k2 (0), p2 (0), k3 (1), p1, k4, p18, k4, p1, k1, p1, k2, p2, k3, p2, k2, p1, k2, [p1, k1] twice.
2nd row [K1, p1] 3 times, k2, p2, k2, p1, k2, p2, k2, p1, k1, p4, k1, [kpk, p3tog] 4 times, k1, p4, k1, p2 (1), k2 (1), p2 (0), k2 (0), [k1, p2, k2, p1, k2, p2, k2] 2 (3) times.
3rd row [K1, p2, k2, p3, k2, p2] 2 (3) times, k1, p2 (0), k2 (0), p2 (0), k1, p1, C4F, p18, C4F, p1, k2, p2, k2, p3, k2, p2, k3, [p1, k1] twice.
4th row [K1, p1] 3 times, p2, k2, p2, k1, p2, k2, p3, k1, p4, k1, [p3tog, kpk] 4 times, k1, p4, k1, p1 (2), k1 (0), p2 (0), k2 (0), p2 (0), [p1, k2, p2, k1, p2, k2, p2] 2 (3) times.
These 4 rows form the patt and are repeated throughout.
Cont in patt until front matches Back to shoulder, ending at armhole edge with a 2nd row.
Shape shoulder
Next row (right side) Cast off 27 (33) sts, with one st on needle after cast off, slip this st and rem 52 sts onto a holder.

RIGHT FRONT
With 4.50mm (US 7) needles, cast on 78 (84) sts.
1st moss st row (right side) [K1, p1] to end.
2nd moss st row [P1, k1] to end.
Rep these 2 rows once more then the 1st row again.
Inc row Moss st 34 (40), [m1, moss st 22] twice. 80 (86) sts.
Change to 5mm (US 8) needles.
1st row (right side) K1, [p1, k1] twice, k1, p1, k2, p2, k3, p2, k2, p1, k1, p1, k4, p18, k4, p1, k3 (1), p2 (0), k2 (0), p1, [k2, p2, k3, p2, k2, p1] 2 (3) times.
2nd row [K2, p2, k2, p1, k2, p2, k1] 2 (3) times, k2 (0), p2 (0), k2 (1), p2 (1), k1, p4, k1, [p3tog, kpk] 4 times, k1, p4, k1, p1, k2, p2, k2, p1, k2, p2, [p1, k1] 3 times.
3rd row K1, [p1, k1] twice, k2, p2, k2, p3, k2, p2, k2, p1, C4B, p18, C4B, p1, k1, p2 (0), k2 (0), p2 (0), k1, [p2, k2, p3, k2, p2, k1] 2 (3) times.
4th row [P2, k2, p2, k1, p2, k2, p1] 2 (3) times, p2, k2 (0), p2 (0), k1 (0), p1 (0), k1, p4, k1, [kpk, p3tog] 4 times, k1, p4, k1, p3, k2, p2, k1, p2, k2, p2, [p1, k1] 3 times.

Herringbone & Cable Jacket

These 4 rows form the patt and are repeated throughout.
Cont in patt until front matches Back to shoulder, ending at armhole edge with a 1st row.

Shape shoulder

Next row (wrong side) Cast off 27 (33) sts, patt to end.
Leave rem 53 sts on a holder – do not break yarn.

NECK EDGE

Join shoulder seams.
Slip all sts from Right Front, Back and Left Front onto a 4.5mm (US 7) circular needle.

1st row (right side) Patt first 48 sts of right front, k1, p2, k1, k last st tog with first st of back, k1, p2, k1, patt across next 49 sts of back, k1, p2, k1, k last st tog with first st of left front, k1, p1, k1, then patt across rem 48 sts of left front. 163 sts.

2nd row Patt 48, p1, k1, p2, k1, p2, k1, p1, patt 49, p1, k1, p2, k1, p2, k1, p1, patt 48.

3rd row Patt 48, k3, p3, k3, patt 49, k3, p3, k3, patt 48.

4th row Patt 48, p2, k2, p1, k2, p2, patt 49, p2, k2, p1, k2, p2, patt 48.
These 4 rows continue the patt on the back and fronts and form the small herringbone patt on the shoulder line and are repeated.
Cont in patt until neck edge measures 5cm/2in from shoulder, ending with a right side cable row of the 4-st cables that outline the centre back panel.

1st dec row (wrong side) Patt 22, p2tog, patt 20, p2tog, patt 14, p2tog, patt 9, [p2tog] twice, k2tog, [p2tog] twice, k1, [p2tog] twice, k2tog, [p2tog] twice, patt 9, p2tog, patt 14, p2tog, patt 20, p2tog, patt 22. 147 sts.

2nd dec row [K1, p1] 13 times, [k2tog, p2tog] 4 times, [k1, p1] 31 times, k1, [p2tog, k2tog] 4 times, [p1, k1] 13 times. 131 sts.
Cont in moss st as set and work a further 5 rows.
Cast off in moss st.

SLEEVES

With 4.50mm (US 7) needles, cast on 43 sts.
Work 5 rows in moss st.
Change to 5mm (US 8) needles and work in herringbone patt as follows,

1st row (right side) * [P1, k2] twice, p2, k3, p1; rep from * to last 7 sts, p1, [k2, p1] twice.

2nd row P2, k3, p2, * k2, p1, k2, p2, k3, p2; rep from * to end.

3rd row * K1, p2, k1, p2, k2, p3, k1; rep from * to last 7 sts, k1, [p2, k1] twice.

4th row K2, p3, k2, * p2, k1, p2, k2, p3, k2; rep from * to end.
These 4 rows form the patt and are repeated.
Inc and take into patt, 1 st at each end of 11th (9th) row and every foll 5th row until there are 75 (79) sts.
Cont straight in patt until sleeve measures 45 (46)cm/17¾ (18)in, ending with a wrong side row.
Cast off.

TO MAKE UP

Matching center of cast off edge of sleeve to shoulder, sew on sleeves. Join side and sleeve seams. ❊

notes

❊ This jacket is designed to give a neat fit across the back, the fronts can be pinned or left to fall open.

Multi-Texture Throw

Treat yourself to a super-soft lace and cable throw in a cashmere mix.

SIZE
Approximately
71 x 104cm/28 x 41 in

MATERIALS
● 12 x 50g balls of Debbie
Bliss Cashmerino Aran in
Silver 027.
● Long 5mm (US 8) circular
needle.
● Cable needle.

TENSION
■ 25 sts and 26 rows to
10cm/4in square over cable
and rib patt using 5mm
(US 8) needles.

PATTERN PANEL
Worked over 11 sts.
1st row (wrong side) P2, [k1, p2] 3 times.
2nd row K2, p1, Cr5L, p1, k2.
3rd row As 1st row.
4th row Cr3LP, k2, p1, k2, Cr3RP.
5th row K1, [p4, k1] twice.
6th row P1, [C4B, p1] twice.
7th row As 5th row.
8th row Cr3RP, k2, p1, k2, Cr3LP.
These 8 rows form the patt panel and are repeated.

TO MAKE
With 5mm (US 8) circular needle, cast on 164 sts.
1st row (right side) K7, * p1, k4, p1, k2, [p2, k2] twice;
rep from * to last 13 sts, p1, k4, p1, k7.
2nd row K8, * p4, k1, p2, [k2, p2] twice, k1; rep
from * to last 12 sts, p4, k8.
3rd row K7, * p1, C4B, p1, k2, [p2, k2] twice; rep from * to
last 13 sts, p1, C4B, p1, k7.
4th row As 2nd row.
These 4 rows form the cable and rib patt with garter st edge
sts and are repeated twice more.
Inc row (right side) K7, [p1, k4, p1, k2, p2, k1, m1, k1, p2,
k2] 9 times, p1, k4, p1, k7. 173 sts.
Now work in patt as follows,
1st row (wrong side) K8, [p4, k1, p11, k1, p4, k13] 4 times,
p4, k1, p11, k1, p4, k8.
2nd row K7, [p1, C4B, p1, k1, yf, k2, ssk, k2tog, k2, yf, k2, p1,
C4B, p1, k11] 4 times, p1, C4B, p1, k1, yf, k2, ssk, k2tog, k2, yf,
k2, p1, C4B, p1, k7.
3rd row As 1st row.
4th row K7, [p1, k4, p1, k2, yf, k2, ssk, k2tog, k2, yf, k1, p1, k4, p1,
k11] 4 times, p1, k4, p1, k2, yf, k2, ssk, k2tog, k2, yf, k1, p1, k4, p1, k7.
5th to 16th rows Rep 1st to 4th rows 3 times more.

abbreviations

Cr3LP = slip next 2 sts
onto cable needle
and hold to front of
work, p1, then k2
from cable needle.
Cr3RP = slip next st
onto cable needle
and hold at back of
work, k2, then p1
from cable needle.
C4B = slip next 2 sts
onto cable needle
and hold at back of
work, k2, then k2
from cable needle.
Cr5L = sl next 3 sts
onto cable needle
and hold to front of
work, k2, sl p st back
onto left hand needle,
p1, then k2 from
cable needle.
Also see page 123.

Multi-Texture Throw

17th row (wrong side) K8, * p4, [k1, p1] 6 times, k1, p4, k1, work across 1st row of patt panel, k1; rep from * 3 times more, p4, [k1, p1] 6 times, k1, p4, k8.

18th row K7, * p1, C4B, p1, [k1, p1] 6 times, C4B, p1, work across 2nd row of patt panel; rep from * 3 times more, p1, C4B, p1, [k1, p1] 6 times, C4B, p1, k7.

19th row K8, * p4, k2, [p1, k1] 5 times, k1, p4, k1, work across 3rd row of patt panel, k1; rep from * 3 times more, p4, k2, [p1, k1] 5 times, k1, p4, k8.

20th row K7, * p1, k4, p2, [k1, p1] 5 times, p1, k4, p1, work across 4th row of patt panel; rep from * 3 times more, p1, k4, p2, [k1, p1] 5 times, p1, k4, p1, k7.

21st row K8, * p4, [k1, p1] 6 times, k1, p4, k1, work across 5th row of patt panel, k1; rep from * 3 times more, p4, [k1, p1] 6 times, k1, p4, k8.

22nd row K7, * p1, C4B, p1, [k1, p1] 6 times, C4B, p1, work across 6th row of patt panel; rep from * 3 times more, p1, C4B, p1, [k1, p1] 6 times, C4B, p1, k7.

23rd row K8, * p4, k2, [p1, k1] 5 times, k1, p4, k1, work across 7th row of patt panel, k1; rep from * 3 times more, p4, k2, [p1, k1] 5 times, k1, p4, k8.

24th row K7, * p1, k4, p2, [k1, p1] 5 times, p1, k4, p1, work across 8th row of patt panel; rep from * 3 times more, p1, k4, p2, [k1, p1] 5 times, p1, k4, p1, k7.

25th to 32nd rows Rep 17th to 24th rows once more.

The last 32 rows form the patt and are repeated 7 times more, ending with a 32nd patt row.

Dec row (wrong side) K8, * p4, k1, p2, k2, p2tog, p1, k2, p2, k1; rep from * to last 12 sts, p4, k8.

Next row K7, * p1, C4B, p1, k2, [p2, k2] twice; rep from * to last 13 sts, p1, C4B, p1, k7.

Next row K8, * p4, k1, p2, [k2, p2] twice, k1; rep from * to last 12 sts, p4, k8.

Next row K7, * p1, k4, p1, k2, [p2, k2] twice;

rep from * to last 13 sts, p1, k4, p1, k7.

Next row K8, * p4, k1, p2, [k2, p2] twice, k1; rep from * to last 12 sts, p4, k8.

The last 4 rows form the cable and rib patt with garter st edge sts and are repeated twice more, then the first of these 4 rows again, so ending with a right side row.

Cast off in patt, working p2tog across center 2 sts of each cable. ✻

Bobble & Cable Sweater

Take a classic Aran and give it a modern edge with a decorative edging.

TO FIT BUST
81–86, 92–97, 102–107 cm
32–34, 36–38, 40–42 in

FINISHED MEASUREMENTS
BUST
94, 104, 124 cm
37, 41, 49 in

LENGTH TO SHOULDER
(including edging)
61, 64, 67 cm
24, 25½, 26½ in

SLEEVE LENGTH
32, 33, 34 cm
(including edging)
12½, 13, 13½ in

MATERIALS
● 14 (16, 17) 50g balls of
Debbie Bliss Cashmerino DK
in Dark Olive Green 31.
● Pair each 3.75mm (US 5)
and 4mm (US 6) knitting
needles.
● 3.75mm (US 5) and
4mm (US 6) circular needles.
● Cable needle.

TENSION
■ 22 sts and 28 rows to
10cm/4in square over st st
using 4mm (US 6) needles.

PANEL A (worked over 9 sts)
1st row (right side) P2, Cr5B, p2.
2nd row K2, p2, k1, p2, k2.
3rd row P1, C3BP, p1, C3FP, p1.
4th row K1, p2, k3, p2, k1.
5th row C3BP, p3, C3FP.
6th row P2, k5, p2.
7th row K2, p2, work [k into front, back and front
of work, turn, k3, turn, p3, turn, k3, turn, sl 1, k2tog,
psso] all into next st, p2, k2.
8th row P2, k5, p2.
9th row C3FP, p3, C3BP.
10th row K1, p2, k3, p2, k1.
11th row P1, C3FP, p1, C3BP, p1.
12th row K2, p2, k1, p2, k2.
These 12 rows form Panel A and are repeated throughout.

PANEL B (worked over 14 sts)
1st row (right side) [K2, p1] 4 times, k2.
2nd, 4th and 6th row [P2, k1] 4 times, p2.
3rd row K2, [p1, Cr5F] twice.
5th row As 1st row.
7th row [Cr5B, p1] twice, k2.
8th row [P2, k1] 4 times, p2.
These 8 rows form Panel B and are repeated throughout.

PANEL C (worked over 8 sts)
1st row (right side) P2, k4, p2.
2nd row K2, p4, k2.
3rd row P2, C4F, p2.
4th row As 2nd row.
These 4 rows form Panel C and are repeated throughout.

PANEL D (worked over 8 sts)
1st row (right side) P2, k4, p2.
2nd row K2, p4, k2.
3rd row P2, C4B, p2.

abbreviations

C4B = slip next 2 sts onto
cable needle and hold
at back of work, k2, then k2
from cable needle.
C4F = slip next 2 sts onto
cable needle and hold
to front of work, k2, then k2
from cable needle.
C3BP = slip next st onto
cable needle and hold
at back of work, k2, then p1
from cable needle.
C3FP = slip next 2 sts onto
cable needle and hold
to front of work, p1, then k2
from cable needle.
Cr5F = slip next 3 sts onto
cable needle and hold
to front of work, k2, slip the
3rd st from cable needle
back on left hand needle,
p this st, then k2 from
cable needle.
Cr5B = slip next 3 sts onto cable
needle and hold at back of
work, k2, slip the 3rd st from
cable needle back on left hand
needle, p this st, then k2 from
cable needle.
MB = make bobble, [p1, yo,
p1, yo, p1] all into next st,
turn, k5, turn, p5, turn, skpo,
k1, k2tog, turn, p3tog.
Also see page 123.

Bobble & Cable Sweater

4th row As 2nd row.

These 4 rows form Panel D and are repeated throughout.

PANEL E (worked over 26 sts)

1st row (right side) P4, [C3BP, C3FP] 3 times, p4.

2nd row K4, p2, [k2, p4] twice, k2, p2, k4.

3rd row P3, C3BP, [p2, C4B] twice, p2, C3FP, p3.

4th, 6th, 8th, 10th, 12th, 16th, 20th and 24th rows K all the
k sts and p the p sts.

5th row P2, C3BP, p2, [C3BP, C3FP] twice, p2, C3FP, p2.

7th row P1, [C3BP, p2] twice, C4F, [p2, C3FP] twice, p1.

9th row [C3BP, p2] twice, C3BP, C3FP, [p2, C3FP] twice.

11th row [K2, p3] twice, k2, p2, k2, [p3, k2] twice.

13th row [C3FP, p2] twice, C3FP, C3BP, [p2, C3BP] twice.

14th row Patt 13, pick up bar between next 2 sts,
work MB in this 'st', place bobble on right side of work, k1, pass
bobble st over this st, patt 12.

15th row P1, [C3FP, p2] twice, C4F, [p2, C3BP] twice, p1.

17th row P2, C3FP, p2, [Cr3F, C3BP] twice, p2, C3BP, p2.

18th row Patt 13, pick up bar between next 2 sts,
work a bobble in this 'st', place bobble on right side of work, k1,
pass bobble st over this st, patt 12.

19th row P3, C3FP, [p2, C4B] twice, p2, C3BP, p3.

21st row P4, [C3FP, C3BP] 3 times, p4.

22nd row Patt 13, pick up bar between next 2 sts,
work a bobble in this 'st', place bobble on right side of work, k1,
pass bobble st over this st, patt 12.

23rd row P5, [C4F, p2] twice, C4F, p5.

25th row P4, [C3BP, C3FP] 3 times, p4.

26th row K4, p2, k2, p4, k1, pick up bar between next 2 sts,
work a bobble in this 'st', place bobble on right side of work, k1,
pass bobble st over this st, p4, k2, p2, k4.

The 3rd to 26th rows form Panel E and are repeated throughout.

BACK AND FRONT (both alike)

With 4mm (US 6) needles, cast on 154 (170, 186) sts.

1st row Work across 1st row of Panel C 1(2, 3) times, then work
across 1st row of Panels A, D, B, C, A, D, E, C, A, D, B, C, A, then
work across 1st row of Panel D 1(2, 3) times.

2nd row Work across 2nd row of Panel D 1 (2, 3) times, then work
across 2nd row of Panels A, C, B, D, A, C, E, D, A, C, B, D, A, then
work across 2nd row of Panel C 1(2, 3) times.

These 2 rows set the position for the patt panels.

Cont in patt until work measures 16cm/6¼in from cast on edge,

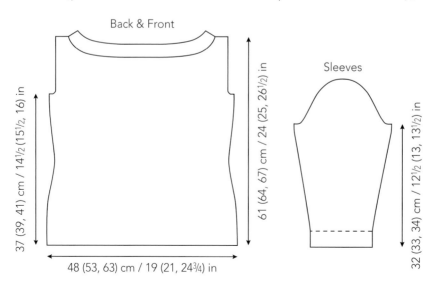

Back & Front

37 (39, 41) cm / 14½ (15½, 16) in

61 (64, 67) cm / 24 (25, 26½) in

48 (53, 63) cm / 19 (21, 24¾) in

Sleeves

32 (33, 34) cm / 12½ (13, 13½) in

Bobble & Cable Sweater

ending with a wrong side row.

Change to 3.75mm (US 5) needles.

Work 24 rows in patt.

Change to 4mm (US 6) needles.

Cont in patt until work measures 37 (39, 41)cm/14½ (15 ¼, 16)in from cast on edge, ending with a wrong side row.

Shape armholes

Cast off 6 sts at beg of next 2 rows. 142 (158, 174) sts.

Work straight until work measures 45 (48, 51)cm/17¾ (19, 20)in from cast on edge, ending with a wrong side row.

Shape neck

Next row Patt 38 (44, 50), turn and work on these sts only for first side of neck, leave rem sts on a spare needle.

Next row Cast off 3 (4, 5) sts, patt to end.

Next row Patt to end.

Rep the last 2 rows twice more. 29 (32, 35) sts

Next row Cast off 2 sts, patt to end.

Next row Patt to end.

Rep the last 2 rows twice more. 23 (26, 29) sts

Dec one st at neck edge of next 5 rows and 3 foll alt rows. 15 (18, 21) sts.

Work 9 rows.

Cast off.

With right side facing, rejoin yarn to rem sts on spare needle, cast off 66 (70, 74) sts, patt to end.

Next row Patt to end.

Next row Cast off 3 (4, 5) sts, patt to end.

Next row Patt to end.

Rep the last 2 rows twice more. 29 (32, 35) sts

Next row Cast off 2 sts, patt to end.

Next row Patt to end.

Rep the last 2 rows twice more. 23 (26, 29) sts

Dec one st at neck edge of next 5 rows and 3 foll alt rows. 15 (18, 21) sts.

Work 9 rows straight.

Cast off.

SLEEVES

With 4mm (US 6) needles, cast on 66 (70, 74) sts.

1st row (right side) P1(3, 5), work across 1st row of Panels C, A, D, B, C, A, D, p1(3, 5).

2nd row K1(3, 5), work across 2nd row of Panels D, A, C, B, D, A, C, k1(3, 5)

These 2 rows set the position for the patt panels, with reverse st st to each side.

Cont in patt, working correct patt panel rows and inc one st at each end of the next row and every foll 6th row until there are 90 (94, 98) sts, working extra sts into reverse st st.

Cont straight until sleeve measures 26 (27, 28)cm/10¼ (10¾, 11)in from cast on edge, ending with a wrong side row.

Shape sleeve top

Cast off 6 sts at beg of next 2 rows. 78 (82, 86) sts.

Dec one st at each end of the next 9 rows then at each end of 5 (6, 7) foll alt rows. 50 (52, 54) sts.

Cast off 2 sts at beg of next 4 rows, then 3 sts at beg of next 8 rows.

Cast off rem 18 (20, 22) sts.

NECK EDGING

Join shoulder seams.

With 3.75mm (US 5) circular needle, pick up and k31 sts down left front neck, 47 (50, 53) sts from front neck, pick up and k30 sts up right front neck, 31 sts down right back neck, 47 (50, 53) sts from back neck, pick up and k30 sts up left back neck. 216 (222, 228) sts.

1st round P to end.

2nd and 3rd rounds K to end.

4th rounds [MB, k2] to end.

5th and 6th round K to end.

7th round P to end.

8th, 9th and 10th rounds [P2, k4] to end.

11th round [P2, C4B] to end.

12th to 15th rounds As 8th to 11th rounds.

16th round As 8th round.

17th round [P0(2, 0), p2tog] to end. 108 (112, 114) sts.

18th, 19th and 20th rounds K to end.

Bobble & Cable Sweater

21st round P to end.

22nd round K to end.

Cast off round K1, [return st to left hand needle, cast on 2 sts, cast off 4 sts] to end, ending last rep cast off 3 sts.

LOWER BORDER

Join side seams.

With 4mm (US 6) circular needle, pick up and k201 (225, 249) sts evenly around lower edge.

1st round P to end.

2nd and 3rd rounds K to end.

4th rounds [MB, k2] to end.

5th round K to end, dec (dec, inc) 1(5, 1) sts evenly. 200 (220, 250) sts.

6th round K to end.

7th round P to end.

8th round [P2, k1, m1, k2] to end. 240 (264, 300) sts.

9th and 10th rounds [P2, k4] to end.

11th round [P2, C4B] to end.

12th round [P2, k4] to end.

13th to 16th rounds As 9th to 12th rounds.

17th round [P3, p2tog, p1] to end. 200 (220, 250) sts.

18th, 19th and 20th rounds K to end.

21st round P to end.

22nd round K to end.

Cast off round K1, [return st to left hand needle, cast on 2 sts, cast off 4 sts] to end, ending last rep cast off 3 sts.

SLEEVE BORDER

Join sleeve seams.

With 4mm (US 6) circular needle, pick up and k51 (57, 63) sts evenly around lower edge.

1st round P to end.

2nd and 3rd rounds K to end.

4th rounds [MB, k2] to end.

5th round K to end, dec (inc, dec) 1 (3, 3) sts evenly. 50 (60, 60) sts.

6th round K to end.

7th round P to end.

8th round [P2, k1, m1, k2] to end. 60 (72, 72) sts.

9th and 10th rounds [P2, k4] to end.

11th round [P2, C4B] to end.

12th round [P2, k4] to end.

13th to 16th rounds As 9th to 12th rounds.

17th round [P3, p2tog, p1] to end. 50 (60, 60) sts.

18th, 19th and 20th rounds K to end.

21st round P to end.

22nd round K to end.

Cast off round K1, [return st to left hand needle, cast on 2 sts, cast off 4 sts] to end, ending last rep cast off 3 sts.

TO MAKE UP

Sew sleeves into armholes easing to fit. ✳

4 designing for kids

designing for kids

When I had my first child, Bill, I had been designing adult hand-knits for magazines for some years. When I became a mother, I wanted to knit for him. What had previously been a rewarding career took on another dimension. I felt the connectedness of knitting, the idea of a craft being handed down over generations, usually by women. Practicality was key, of course, but through their hands, knitters have always been able to invest their garments with the love they feel for their recipients. As such, knitting has long been associated with warmth and comfort, what the Danish call "hygge" (HOO-gah), the sense of hearth and home.

There will always be something particularly special about knitting for a new baby, whether knitting while pregnant or making something for family or friends. If there's any time between work projects, there's nothing I like better than making something for a little one. As I write this, I'm working on a small project to welcome home my new great-nephew. It is a very simple top with a hood just like one his father wears, but by working his initial, F for Frankie, on the front, I have personalized it **(A)**. I'm sure that his parents will treasure it, because they know I put time aside to make it especially for him and that each stitch represents the love I have for them and the new addition to our family. If knit in good-quality yarn and treated with care, a hand knit can often be passed down to the next baby in the family, and so its story carries on. A tiny garment or booties can also be framed and kept as a reminder of that special time.

Knitting for babies is also the perfect way for a beginner or lapsed knitter to get into the craft. Large projects can be overwhelming, and the length of time it takes to complete a garment can make the initial enthusiasm soon evaporate. Buying a few balls of yarn and a simple pattern is manageable, and a baby item can be finished in days or weeks rather than months. Baby garments are also portable—there is something so satisfying about taking a small piece of knitting with you to knit in the car or train or on your lunch hour.

When Bill was born there were very few contemporary-looking knits for babies; designs were still firmly stuck in the lacy layette styles of previous generations, with fussy coats, bonnets and shawls worked in fine yarns in sickly pastels or white. Even twenty years ago, using primary colors or navy was considered very off-the-wall. Lace was popular, but

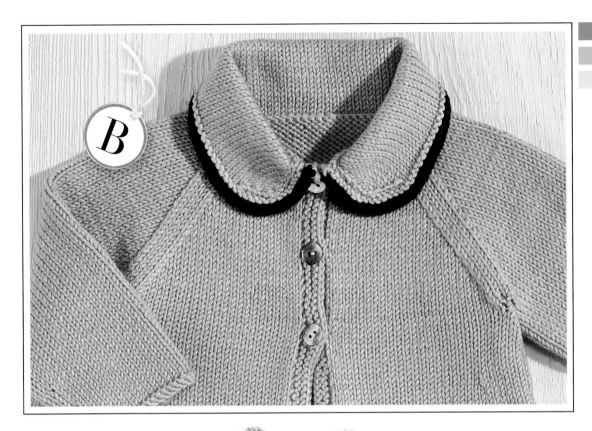

83

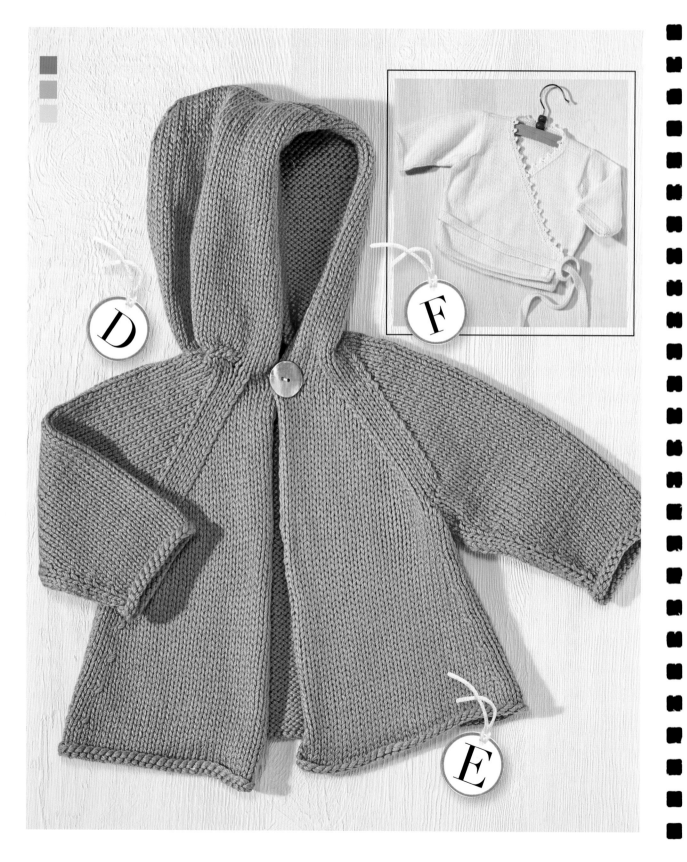

designing for kids

I've always seen the fabric as holes waiting to trap small fingers. As a designer, I wanted to create more modern styles, with pared-down shapes and detailing creating the interest. It soon became clear, however, that there was a world of difference between designing for babies and designing for adults.

I learned that practicality was essential. Anyone who has had a colicky infant will know a miserable baby doesn't want to be changed or handled too much. Front openings wouldn't get trapped over his head, so I began to design cardigans and jackets or sweaters with button fastenings on the shoulders or back of the neck. At the time, we were taught to lay babies on their sides, but these days the safest position is considered to be on their backs. Consequently, this has changed how I design. Because buttons can be hard against such new skin, I now avoid back-of-the-neck openings or crossover tops that tie at the back. It is important, too, to avoid embellishments such as ties or pompoms that can come off and be swallowed. Hairy yarns such as angora or mohair should not be used—the loose fibers can be ingested or inhaled.

When designing for adults, I am aware of body shape as well as fashion trends, but babies and children are basically tube-shaped. A-lines or triangular shapes work well not only because they are a sweet style on babies and small children but also because they go over bulky diapers. Crossover ballerina-style cardigans are also very useful to a new mother, since they can be easily tied without trying to fasten fiddly buttons. It is also important that there aren't tight ribs that go across the midriff or around the wrists—you don't want to struggle to pull the garment down or get delicate hands through the cuffs. I often work a small

side-vent at the lower hems on the body to make a garment roomier. The thumb method of cast-on is preferable on lower edges—it has the most elasticity.

Children always have the most adorable faces, and I like to include features that bring the eye up to those beautifully rounded cheeks. A collar framing the face is perfect. I love neat Peter Pan collars such as the one here **(B)** on a design that appeared in *Vogue Knitting*. Shawl collars are also a perfect style for both boys and girls, and can be further prettified for a girl by ending with a picot edge. A very simple garment can be transformed by a decorative collar **(C)**. This edging, worked by creating small triangles of moss stitch, can be used at the end of a sleeve, as an alternative to a button band, or at the hem of the garment.

Because it is preferable to keep the shapes of children's designs simple, it can give the designer the opportunity to introduce small details that keep the garments from looking too boring. It might be a little bit of fully fashioned shaping of the raglan on a jacket or around a neck that breaks up the plain fabric **(D)**, a

designing for kids

roll edging rather than rib on a hem **(E)**, or just a snuggly hood. A pretty edging can look sweet on a girl's crossover cardigan to make it different from the classic ballerina style **(F)**, and a ribbon tie or a touch of embroidery on a collar add interest to an otherwise classic cardigan.

Children are magpies, so a pocket on a design is perfect for storing away a small toy or coins to buy a treat. It doesn't always have to be on the body—it can go on a sleeve, and the pocket lining can be in a contrast shade. A pocket can also break up a large "slab" of fabric as in the Smock Dress, page 88.

Knitting for children is also a wonderful opportunity to involve them in the craft. I have met many disappointed knitters who wonder why they never see their grandchildren in the garments they knitted for them, but never ask themselves whether the child wanted to wear a tight-fitting, scratchy Aran sweater in cream. It is a great time to introduce a child to the magic of making things; to a kid, a yarn store can look like an Aladdin's cave, full of color and textures. Let the child choose the style, color or buttons, or customize the garment with initials (see swatch on previous page) or a motif of a favorite animal or toy. Including children in these decisions makes them feel important—plus it is never too early to show them the pleasure of creating a garment rather than buying one!

There are fantastic colors available now, not just primaries and dusky pastels but also greys, terracottas, mossy greens, and, my favorite on children, chocolate brown. I avoid working in primaries, but this is purely subjective. When using brights, I like to go for sharp pinks rather than pillar-box reds. Very strong shades can look hard and draining against delicate young skin.

One of the styles that crops up time after time in my collections is the smock. I make no apologies for this—it's a style I love on many levels. It can have a special, dressed-up look for a little girl, and the gathered yoke is really appealing. However, it is the history of the smock that I love. I was brought up in a rural agricultural area of England, where we were surrounded by "picture book" thatched cottages. My grandmother remembered the farmers coming to chapel in their Sunday-best smocks, the amount of embroidery showing the status of each man (see Smock Dress, page 88).

Details such as dropped shoulders on casual sweaters are good for ease of movement, and, as ever, yarn choice is crucial: For sporty tops you need yarn that creates a fabric that is soft to wear and not scratchy, particularly around the neck. It should also be hard-wearing and machine washable. An extra-fine merino is perfect for these styles (see Boy's Zipped Sweater, page 94). ■

If you want to design an easy sweater for a child:	

▶ Begin by measuring a favorite, very simple style that they feel comfortable in rather than measuring the actual body of the child. This is because the original sweater measurements will give you a size and ease allowance you know the child will like.

▶ The numbers may need to be altered depending on whether you are going to change the weight of yarn or stitch. A heavier yarn needs some extra room, so you will need to allow for this by adding to the measurements.

▶ Choose a dropped shoulder so that you don't have to worry about sleeve and armhole shaping. Work a gauge swatch and find out the number of stitches and rows to 4 inches. When you know how many stitches you have to the inch, you can work out how many stitches and rows you need to knit your sweater.

patterns

Here are three of my favorite design choices in children's wear.

Smock Dress

Somewhere there is a picture of my great-great-grandfather wearing a smocked tunic in a church choir stall. My husband, Barry, bought me one for my birthday one year, and it takes pride of place in my studio and is pictured here on page 88. For this reason I have included a smock dress in the collection. Knitted in Prima, my wool/bamboo yarn that drapes beautifully, the stitch patterning on the yoke, collar and tops of the sleeves echoes the embroidery on the original one, and I have used the traditional calico shade. The gathering on the front gives a pretty, retro feel.

Zipped Sweater

Because I like to include surprise in my knits, the doubled collar is knit in a contrasting red on the inner side, providing a flash of color. A red stripe on the ribs and a red zipper both tie in with this, while the rib on the yoke breaks up the stockinette stitch for added interest. Zippers can be problematic in knitwear—when the wrong side shows, it will also show the reverse side of the zipper. To disguise this, the doubled-over collar contains the zip within it, and a selvedge has been created by extending the stitches on the collar so that when sewn down it hides the zipper. The yarn is an extra-fine merino in an Aran weight and is light but hard-wearing.

Garter Stitch Jacket with Vent

I worked this jacket in my two favorite contrast shades, pale blue edged with chocolate brown, and I knit it in simple garter stitch with a rolled edge in stocking stitch and a back vent. Contrasting buttons stand out against the background. The yarn is a cashmere mix, the weight between a traditional four-ply and double knitting weight, making it perfect for babies. Because an infant cannot tell us if a fabric is uncomfortable, it is crucial to knit with fibers that are gentle on a baby's skin. I like to use my extra-fine merino, cashmere and microfiber mixes, which combine softness and washability.

Smock Dress

One of my favorite styles—a smock dress inspired by a 19th-century English farmer's smock. Gently pleated, it gets a fashionable update with a decorative yoke and pockets.

TO FIT AGES
3–6, 6–12, 12–18, 18–24 months

FINISHED MEASUREMENTS
CHEST
54, 59, 65, 70 cm
21¼, 23¼, 25½, 27½ in

LENGTH
36, 39, 43, 50 cm
14¼, 15¼, 17, 19¾ in

SLEEVE SEAM
18, 20, 22, 24 cm
7, 8, 8¾, 9½ in

MATERIALS
● 6 (7, 8, 9) 50g balls Debbie Bliss Prima in Stone 05.
● Pair each 3.25mm (US 3), 3.75mm (US 5) and 4mm (US 6) knitting needles.
● Short 3.25mm (US 3) circular needle.
● One button.

TENSION
■ 22 sts and 30 rows to 10cm/4in square over st st using 4mm (US 6) needles.

ABBREVIATIONS
See page 123.

BACK
With 3.25mm (US 3) needles, cast on 92 (98, 104, 110) sts.
K 5 rows.
Change to 4mm (US 6) needles.
Beg with a k row, work in st st until back measures 19 (21, 25, 31)cm/7½ (8¼, 10, 12¼)in from cast on edge, ending with a k row.
Next row P15 (18, 21, 24), [p2tog] 31 times, p15 (18, 21, 24); 61 (67, 73, 79) sts
Change to 3.75mm (US 5) needles and work in patt as follows:
1st row (right side) K15 (18, 21, 24), work across 1st row of Chart, k15 (18, 21, 24).
2nd row P15 (18, 21, 24), work across 2nd row of Chart, p15 (18, 21, 24).
These 2 rows set the position of the chart with st st to each side.
Cont in patt until back measures 26 (28, 31, 37)cm/10¼ (11, 12¼, 14½)in from cast on edge, ending with a wrong side row.

Shape armholes
Cast off 6 sts at beg of next 2 rows. 49 (55, 61, 67) sts.
Cont in patt until all 48 chart rows have been worked, so ending with a wrong side row. **

Divide for back opening
Next row K25 (28, 31, 34), turn and work on these sts only for first side of neck opening, leave rem sts on a spare needle.
Next row K2, p to end.
Next row K to end.
Rep the last 2 rows until back measures 36 (39, 43, 50)cm/14 (15¼, 17, 19¾)in from cast on edge, ending with a wrong side row.

notes
✳ I received this dress from my husband as a Christmas gift some years ago. It dates back to the mid-19th century and comes from Bedfordshire, the county in which I was born and grew up. It's been the source of inspiration for many of my designs, and variations of it have often been included in my children's collections.

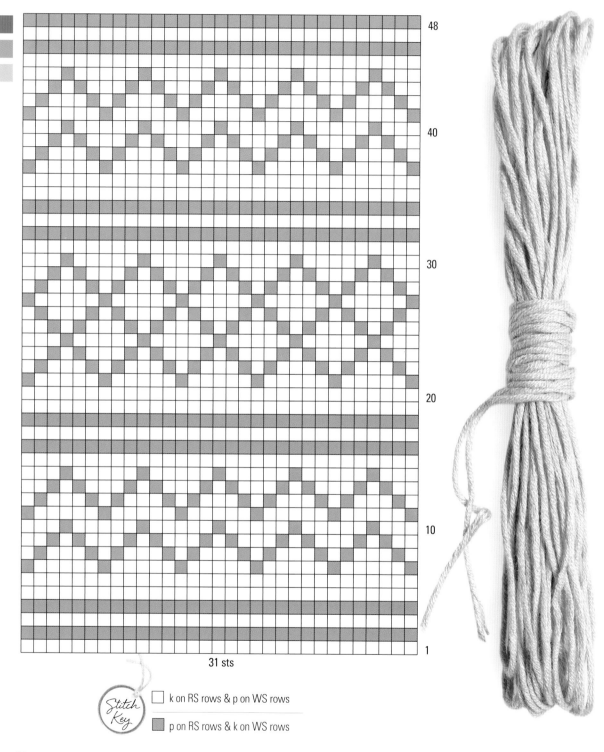

48

40

30

20

10

1

31 sts

Stitch Key

☐ k on RS rows & p on WS rows

▨ p on RS rows & k on WS rows

Smock Dress

Shape shoulder

Next row Cast off 7 (8, 9, 10) sts, k to end.
Next row K2, p to end.
Next row Cast off 8 (9, 10, 11) sts, k to end.
Next row K2, p to end.
Leave rem 10 (11, 12, 13) sts on a holder.
With right side facing, cast on one st, then k sts on spare needle.
Next row P to last 2 sts, k2.
Next row K to end.
Rep the last 2 rows until back measures 36 (39, 43, 50)cm/14 (15¼, 17, 19¾)in from cast on edge, ending with a right side row.

Shape shoulder

Next row Cast off 7 (8, 9, 10) sts, p to last 2 sts, k2.
Next row K to end.
Next row Cast off 8 (9, 10, 11) sts, p to last 2 sts, k2.
Next row K to end.
Leave rem 10 (11, 12, 13) sts on a holder.

FRONT

Work as given for Back to **. 49 (55, 61, 67) sts.

Shape neck

Next row (right side) K18 (20, 22, 24) sts, turn and work on these sts only for first side of neck shaping, leave rem sts on spare needle.
Dec 1 st at neck edge on 3 foll right side rows. 15 (17, 19, 21) sts.
Cont without further shaping until front measures same as Back to shoulder, ending at side edge.

Shape shoulder

Cast off 7 (8, 9, 10) sts at beg of next row.
Work 1 row.
Cast off rem 8 (9, 10, 11) sts.
With right side facing, slip centre 13 (15, 17, 19) sts onto a holder, rejoin yarn to rem sts on a spare needle, k to end.
Complete to match first side, reversing shaping.

POCKETS (both alike)

With 3.75mm (US 5) needles, cast on 17 (17, 23, 23) sts.
K 3 rows.
Change to 4mm (US 6) needles.
1st row (right side) K to end.
2nd row K2, p13 (13, 19, 19), k2.
Rep the last 2 rows 6 (6, 8, 8) times more.
Change to 3.75mm (US 5) needles.
Next row (right side) K2, work across first 13 (13, 19, 19) sts of 1st row of Chart, k2.
Keeping the continuity of garter st border, work next 17 rows from Chart.
Cast off.

SLEEVES

With 3.25mm (US 3) needles, cast on 33 (35, 39, 41) sts.
K 5 rows.
Inc row (right side) K6 (7, 9, 10), [m1, k3] 7 times, m1, k6 (7, 9, 10). 41 (43, 47, 49) sts.
Change to 4mm (US 6) needles.
Beg with a p row, work in st st.
Work 3 (3, 3, 5) rows.
Inc row (right side) K2, m1, k to last 2 sts, m1, k2.
Work 5 rows.
Rep the last 6 rows 4 (5, 6, 7) times more and the inc row again. 53 (57, 63, 67) sts.
Work 1 row.
Dec row P12 (14, 17, 19), [p2tog, p2] 7 times, p2tog, p11 (13, 16, 18). 45 (49, 55, 59) sts.
Change to 3.75mm (US 5) needles.
Next row K7 (9, 12, 14), work across 15th chart row, k7 (9, 12, 14).
Next row P7 (9, 12, 14), work across 16th chart row, p7 (9, 12, 14).
Work a further 12 rows as set.
Place markers at each end of last row.
Work a further 6 rows of chart, so ending with the 34th chart row.
Cast off.

Smock Dress

COLLAR

Join shoulder seams.

With right side facing and 3.25mm (US 3) circular needle, slip 10 (11, 12, 13) sts from left back holder onto needle, pick up and k8 (10, 10, 12) sts down left front neck, k13 (15, 17, 19) sts across centre front neck, pick up and k8 (10, 10, 12) sts up right front neck, then k10 (11, 12, 13) sts from right back holder. 49 (57, 61, 69) sts.

Next row (wrong side) K to end.

Next row K24 (28, 30, 34) sts, cast off one st, k to end. 48 (56, 60, 68) sts.

Next row K24 (28, 30, 34) sts, turn and work on these sts only for first half of collar.

Inc row (right side) K2 (2, 3, 2), [k5 (4, 6, 5), m1] 4 (6, 4, 6) times, m1, k2 (2, 3, 2). 29 (35, 35, 41) sts.

K 1 row.

Change to 3.75mm (US 5) needles.

Next row K2, p to last 2 sts, k2.

Next row K2, work across 20th row chart, k2.

Next row K2, work across 21st row of chart, k2.

Cont as set until 12 chart rows have been worked in total.

Change to 4mm (US 6) needles.

K 4 rows.

Cast off.

With wrong side facing, rejoin yarn to rem sts, k2 (2, 3, 2), [k5 (4, 6, 5), m1] 4 (6, 4, 6) times, m1, k2 (2, 3, 2). 29 (35, 35, 41) sts.

Work second half of collar to match first.

TO MAKE UP

Sew sleeves into armholes, easing to fit, with row ends above markers sewn to sts cast off at underarm. Join side and sleeve seams. Sew on pockets. Make a button loop on left back opening and sew button to right back opening to match. ✳

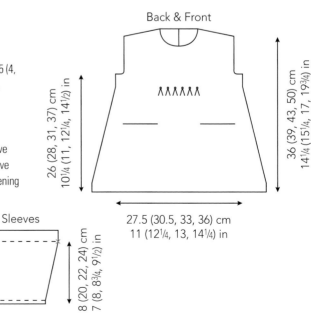

Back & Front

26 (28, 31, 37) cm
10¼ (11, 12¼, 14½) in

36 (39, 43, 50) cm
14¼ (15¼, 17, 19¾) in

27.5 (30.5, 33, 36) cm
11 (12¼, 13, 14¼) in

Sleeves

18 (20, 22, 24) cm
7 (8, 8¾, 9½) in

Zipped Sweater

A child-friendly chunky knit with plenty of wiggle room. Warm and cozy, the contrasting-color zip and sporty style give it total boy-appeal!

TO FIT AGES
2–3, 3–4, 4–5, 5–6 years

FINISHED MEASUREMENTS
CHEST
76, 82, 88, 94 cm
30, 32, 34¾, 37½ in

LENGTH
35, 40, 45, 50 cm
13¾, 15¾, 17¾, 19¾ in

SLEEVE LENGTH
22, 25, 28, 31 cm
8¾, 10, 11, 12¼ in

MATERIALS
● 6 (7, 8, 9) 50g balls of Debbie Bliss Rialto Aran in Chocolate Brown 17 (M) and one 50g ball in Red 18 (C).
● Pair each 4.5mm (US 7) and 5mm (US 8) needles.
● 15cm/6in zipper.

TENSION
■ 18 sts and 24 rows to 10cm/4in square over st st using 5mm (US 8) needles.

BACK
With 4.50mm (US 7) needles and C, cast on 70 (74, 82, 86) sts.
1st row (right side) K2, [p2, k2] to end.
2nd row P2, [k2, p2] to end.
Change to M.
3rd row K to end.
4th row P2, [k2, p2] to end.
5th row K2, [p2, k2] to end.
Rep the last 2 rows 3 (4, 5, 6) times more, then the 4th row again and inc 2 sts evenly across last row on 2nd and 4th sizes only. 70 (76, 82, 88) sts.
Change to 5mm (US 8) needles.
Beg with a k row, work in st st until back measures 20 (24, 29, 33)cm/8 (9½, 11½, 13)in from cast on edge, ending with a k row.
Inc row (wrong side) P3 (8, 7, 6), m1, [p5 (4, 4, 4), m1] 13 (15, 17, 19) times, p2 (8, 7, 6). 84 (92, 100, 108) sts. **
Now work in yoke patt as follows:
1st row K3, [p2, Tw2R, p2, k2] to last 9 sts, p2, Tw2R, p2, k3.
2nd row P3, [k2, p2] to last 5 sts, k2, p3.
Rep the last 2 rows until back measures 35 (40, 45, 50)cm/13¾ (15¾, 17¾, 19¾)in from cast on edge, ending with a p row.
Shape shoulders
Cast off 9 (10, 11, 12) sts at beg of next 4 rows and 8 sts at beg of next 2 rows.
Leave the rem 32 (36, 40, 44) sts on a holder.

FRONT
Work as given for Back to **.
Divide for front opening
1st row (right side) K3, [p2, Tw2R, p2, k2] 4 (5, 5, 6) times, [p2, Tw2R] 1 (0, 1, 0) times, k3, turn and work on these 42 (46, 50, 54) sts for first side of neck shaping, leave rem sts on a holder.
2nd row K3, [p2, k2] to last 3 sts, p3.
Cont in patt as set until front measures 30 (34, 39, 43)cm/11¾ (13½, 15¼, 17)in from cast on edge, ending with a wrong side row.
Shape neck
Next row Patt 34 (37, 40, 43), turn and leave rem 8 (9, 10, 11)

Sleeves

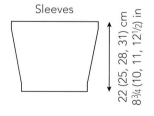

22 (25, 28, 31) cm
8¾ (10, 11, 12½) in

Back & Front

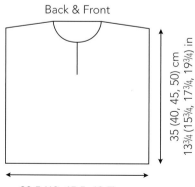

35 (40, 45, 50) cm
13¾ (15¾, 17¾, 19¾) in

38.5 (42, 45.5, 48.5) cm
15¼ (16½, 17¾, 19¼) in

Zipped Sweater

sts on a holder for collar.

Dec one st at neck edge on every row until 26 (28, 30, 32) sts rem.

Cont straight until front measures same as Back to shoulder, ending at side edge.

Shape shoulder

Cast off 9 (10, 11, 12) sts at beg of next and foll alt row.

Work 1 row. Cast off rem 8 sts.

With right side facing, rejoin yarn to rem 42 (46, 50, 54) sts on holder and work as follows,

1st row K3, [Tw2R, p2] 1 (0, 1, 0) times, [k2, p2, Tw2R, p2] 4 (5, 5, 6) times, k3.

2nd row P3, [k2, p2] to last 3 sts, k3.

Cont in patt as set until front measures 30 (34, 39, 43)cm/11¾ (13½, 15¼, 17)in from cast on edge, ending with a wrong side row.

Shape neck

Next row Patt 8 (9, 10, 11) sts and slip these sts onto a holder for collar, patt to end.

Dec one st at neck edge on every row until 26 (28, 30, 32) sts rem.

Cont straight until front measures same as Back to shoulder, ending at side edge.

Shape shoulder

Cast off 9 (10, 11, 12) sts at beg of next and foll alt row.

Work 1 row. Cast off rem 8 sts.

SLEEVES

With 4.50mm (US 7) needles and C, cast on 34 (38, 42, 46) sts.

1st row (right side) K2, [p2, k2] to end.

2nd row P2, [k2, p2] to end.

Change to M.

3rd row K to end.

4th row P2, [k2, p2] to end.

5th row K2, [p2, k2] to end.

Rep the last 2 rows 3 (3, 4, 4) times more and the 4th row again.

Change to 5mm (US 8) needles

Beg with a k row, work in st st.

Work 2 rows.

Inc row K3, m1, k to last 3 sts, m1, k3.

Work 3 rows.

Rep the last 4 rows 7 (8, 9, 10) times more and the inc row again.

52 (58, 64, 70) sts.

Cont in st st until sleeve measures 22 (25, 28, 31)cm/8¾ (10, 11, 12¼)in from cast on edge, ending with a wrong side row.

Cast off.

COLLAR

Join shoulder seams.

With right side facing, 5mm (US 8) needles and M, slip 8 (9, 10, 11) sts from right front holder onto needle, pick up and k20 (21, 22, 23) sts up right front neck, k across 32 (36, 40, 44) sts from back neck holder, pick up and k20 (21, 22, 23) sts down left front neck, then patt across 8 (9, 10, 11) sts from left front. 88 (96, 104, 112) sts.

Next row (wrong side) K3, [p2, k2] to last 5 sts, p2, k3.

Next row K5, [p2, k2] to last 7 sts, p2, k5.

Rep the last 2 rows until collar measures 5cm/2in, ending with a wrong side row.

Change to C.

Change to 4.50mm (US 7) needles.

Next row Cast off 2 sts, k to end.

Next row Cast off 2 sts, rib to end. 84 (92, 100, 108) sts.

Next row (right side) K3, [p2, k2] to last 5 sts, p2, k3.

Next row K1, [p2, k2] to last 3 sts, p2, k1.

Cont in rib with 1 st in garter st at each end for a further 4.5cm/1¾in, ending with a wrong side row.

Next row K4, cast off next 76 (84, 92, 100) sts, k to end.

Cont on last set of 4 sts for first facing strip, leave rem 4 sts on a holder.

Next row (wrong side) K1, p2, k1.

Next row K to end.

Rep the last 2 rows until strip fits down front neck opening edge, ending with a wrong side row.

Cast off.

With wrong side facing, rejoin yarn to rem 4 sts on holder for second facing strip.

Complete to match first side.

TO MAKE UP

With center of cast off edge of sleeve to shoulder, sew on sleeves.

Join side and sleeve seams. Hand sew zipper in place.

Fold collar in half to wrong side and slip st in place. Sew facing strips over zipper tape to neaten. �֍

Garter Stitch Jacket with Vent

A cozy knit in garter stitch with a contrast edging and back vent for ease.

TO FIT AGE
3–6, 6–9, 9–12, 12–18 months

FINISHED MEASUREMENTS
CHEST
52, 57, 62, 67 cm
20½, 22½, 24½, 26½ in

LENGTH TO SHOULDER
(including rolled edging)
25, 27, 29, 33 cm
10, 10¾, 11½, 13 in

SLEEVE LENGTH
(with cuff turned back)
11, 13, 15, 19 cm
4¼, 5, 6, 7½ in

MATERIALS
● 4 (5, 5, 6) 50g balls
of Debbie Bliss Baby
Cashmerino in Pale Blue
202 (M) and one 50g ball in
Chocolate Brown 011 (C).
● Pair each of 3mm (US 2–3)
and 3.25mm (US 3) knitting
needles.
● 3 buttons.

TENSION
■ 25 sts and 50 rows
to 10cm/4in square over
garter st using 3.25mm
(US 3) needles.

ABBREVIATIONS
See page 123.

BACK
Left side lower edging With 3.25mm (US 3) needles and C,
cast on 33 (36, 39, 42) sts.
Beg with a k row, work 4 rows in st st. **
Break yarn and leave these sts on a spare needle.
Right side lower edging Work as Left side
edging to **.
Next row (right side) K33 (36, 39, 42), turn
and cast on 26 sts, k33 (36, 39, 42) sts from first side
edging. 92 (98, 104, 110) sts.
Next row P33 (36, 39, 42), k26, p33 (36, 39, 42).
Change to M.
*** **Next row** (right side) K to end.
Next row K39 (42, 45, 48), sl 1, k12, sl 1, k39 (42, 45, 48).
Next row K32 (35, 38, 41), sl 1, k26, sl 1,
k32 (35, 38, 41). Rep the last 2 rows until back
measures 14 (15, 16, 19)cm/5½ (6, 6¼, 7½)in from ***,
ending with a wrong side row.
Shape armholes
Cast off 4 sts at beg of next 2 rows. 84 (90, 96, 102) sts.
Work a further 14 rows.
Next row K29 (32, 35, 38), cast off 26, k29 (32, 35, 38). 58
(64, 70, 76) sts.
Cont straight until back measures 24 (26, 28, 32)cm/9½ (10¼,
11, 12½)in from ***, ending with a wrong side row.
Shape shoulders
Cast off 7 (8, 9, 10) sts at beg of next 4 rows.
Cast off rem 30 (32, 34, 36) sts.

LEFT FRONT
With 3.25mm (US 3) needles and C, cast on 36(39, 42, 45) sts.
Beg with a k row, work 6 rows st st.
Change to M.
Work in garter st until front measures 14 (15, 16, 19)cm/5½ (6, 6¼,
7½)in from beg of garter st, ending with a wrong side row.

■ See page 143 for Little Buddy jacket instructions

Garter Stitch Jacket with Vent

Shape armhole

Cast off 4 sts at beg of next row. 32 (35, 38, 41) sts.
Cont straight until front measures 20 (22, 24, 27)cm/8 (8¾, 9½, 10¾)in from beg of garter st, ending with a wrong side row.

Shape neck

Next row (right side) K22 (24, 26, 28), turn and work on these sts only, leave rem 10 (11, 12, 13) sts on a holder.
Dec one st at neck edge on 8 foll right side rows. 14 (16, 18, 20) sts.
Cont straight until front measures same as Back to shoulder, ending at armhole edge.

Shape shoulder

Next row Cast off 7 (8, 9, 10) sts, k to end.
K 1 row.
Cast off rem 7 (8, 9, 10) sts.

RIGHT FRONT

Mark position for 3 buttons on left front, the first 13 (13, 14, 14)cm/5 (5, 5½, 5½)in from beg of garter st, the 3rd 1cm/½ in below neck edge with the rem button spaced evenly between.
Work buttonholes to match markers as follows:
Buttonhole row (right side) K3, yf, k2tog, k to end.
With 3.25mm (US 3) needles and C, cast on 36 (39, 42, 45) sts.
Beg with a k row, work 6 rows st st.
Change to M.
Work in garter st until front measures 14 (15, 16, 19)cm/5½ (6, 6¼, 7½)in from beg of garter st, ending with a right side row.

Shape armhole

Cast off 4 sts at beg of next row. 32 (35, 38, 41) sts.
Cont straight until front measures 20 (22, 24, 27)cm/8 (8¾, 9½, 10¾)in from beg of garter st, ending with a wrong side row.

Shape neck

Next row (right side) K10 (11, 12, 13) and leave these sts on a holder, k to end.
Dec one st at neck edge on 8 foll right side rows. 14 (16, 18, 20) sts.
Cont straight until front measures same as Back to shoulder, ending at armhole edge.

Shape shoulder

Next row Cast off 7 (8, 9, 10) sts, k to end.

K 1 row.
Cast off rem 7 (8, 9, 10) sts.

SLEEVES

With 3.25mm (US 3) needles and C, cast on 35 (37, 41, 43) sts.
Beg with a p row, work 5 rows in st st.
Change to M.
K 9 rows.
Place a marker at each end of last row.
K 8 rows.
Inc row (right side) K3, m1, k to last 3 sts, m1, k3.
K 5 rows.
Rep the last 6 rows 3 times more and the inc row again.
45 (47, 51, 53) sts.
Now cont in garter st and inc 1 st as before on every foll 10th (8th, 8th, 8th) row until there are 47 (53, 59, 65) sts.
Cont straight until sleeve measures 11 (13, 15, 19)cm/4¼ (5, 6, 7½)in from markers, ending with a wrong side row.
Place a marker at each end of last row.
K 8 rows.
Cast off.

NECKBAND

Join shoulder seams.
With right side facing, 3mm (US 2-3) needles and M, slip 10 (11, 12, 13) sts from right front neck holder onto a needle, pick up and k12 (13, 14, 15) sts up right front neck, 30 (32, 34, 36) sts from back neck holder, pick up and k12 (13, 14, 15) sts down left side of front neck, then k10 (11, 12, 13) sts from left front holder. 74 (80, 86, 92) sts.
Next row K to end.
Change to C.
Beg with a k row, work 6 rows in st st.
Cast off.

LEFT FRONT BAND

With right side facing, 3mm (US 2-3) needles and C, pick up and k54 (58, 62, 68) sts along garter st row ends of left front edge.
K 1 row. Cast off.

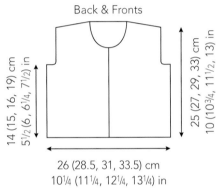

Back & Fronts

14 (15, 16, 19) cm
5½ (6, 6¼, 7½) in

25 (27, 29, 33) cm
10 (10¾, 11½, 13) in

26 (28.5, 31, 33.5) cm
10¼ (11¼, 12¼, 13¼) in

RIGHT FRONT BAND

With right side facing, 3mm (US 2–3) needles and C, pick up and k 54 (58, 62, 68) sts along garter st row ends of right front edge. Beg with a p row, work 5 rows st st.
Cast off.

TO MAKE UP

Matching center of cast off edge of sleeve to shoulder, sew sleeves into armholes, with row ends above markers sewn to sts cast off at underarm. Join side and sleeve seams, reversing seam on contrast lower edges to allow for roll. Fold cuffs up onto right side. Sew on buttons. Fold cast off sts at center back to form a box pleat on wrong side of work and sew in place. Join neckband to front bands. ❉

Sleeves

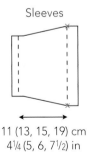

11 (13, 15, 19) cm
4¼ (5, 6, 7½) in

5: designing with details

designing with details

To me, detail in a design can transform something simple into something special. I think that we all pay attention to detail in our lives, whether it's the way we set the table, present food on a plate, or arrange a bedroom for a visitor. In a way, it is about having respect for what you do, making it as pleasing as possible and going that extra mile. A very basic sweater in stockinette stitch is a great project for a beginner. However, a basic design is no reason to shortchange the knitter!

I will take as long to think about a simple design as I would a more complex one. Fully fashioned shaping at the sides and around the neck may give some interest, or I might choose a raglan rather than a set-in sleeve so the diagonal creates a line across the body. In many ways the effects of detailing can be fairly subliminal, but including them makes the difference between a well-thought-out design and a sloppy one.

I really enjoy thinking about what will enhance a design; I let the style and stitch pattern dictate the course things will take. For example, if I were working on a seed stitch jacket, its reversibility would allow a collar to be created by increasing on the fronts and turning back, as on the Garter Stitch Coat (page 16), where the collar folds back over the fronts. This means that there doesn't need to be any pick-up bands on the fronts that would show an ugly seam. Using borders is a great detailing effect: a garter stitch border, which is also reversible, can be integrated into the main pattern as you are working it. A small caveat here: A garter stitch border will only work on a fairly short jacket—on a longer one the discrepancy between the gauges can cause the center front edges to pull up. I may also add pockets to break up the solid effect of the all-over stitch pattern, giving the pocket tops garter stitch borders to match the front bands. I always prefer to use a picked-up horizontal band rather than a vertical one that needs to be sewn on. The reason being that it's very difficult to get a perfect

seam on a vertical band, especially if it is a ribbed one, and the front bands are on view, so they need to look absolutely perfect.

Attention to detail is all about making choices based on what will make the garment as good as it can be. For example, based on my experience of previous garments, I have a standard set of measurements when I am compiling a pattern. I will usually make my neck depth on a classic crewneck about 3 inches. However, if I were working on a sweater with horizontal bands of colorwork, I would want to make sure that the neck doesn't begin too near the last row of Fair Isle. There needs to be at least two clear rows of the main background before the neck begins, because the stitches for the neckband will pull up slightly, distorting the horizontal line of Fair Isle. If I have to make the neck depth slightly higher, I will compensate by making the back neck depth wider so there is still the same amount of space for the head.

Cabled patterns need to be carefully thought out, too, because at the point where the cables cross, the thickness and tension in the fabric can cause the neckband to distort. To avoid this, it is better to make sure the beginning of the neck or the shoulders doesn't coincide with a cable row.

The type of stitch can also dictate the style of sleeve. A set-in sleeve will interfere with a large pattern used on the body, so a dropped shoulder may have to be used instead. I often use a square set-in

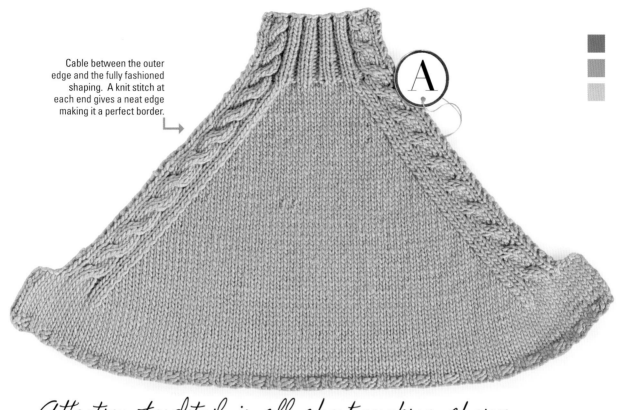

Cable between the outer edge and the fully fashioned shaping. A knit stitch at each end gives a neat edge making it a perfect border.

A

*Attention to detail is all about making choices
to make the garment as good as it can be.*

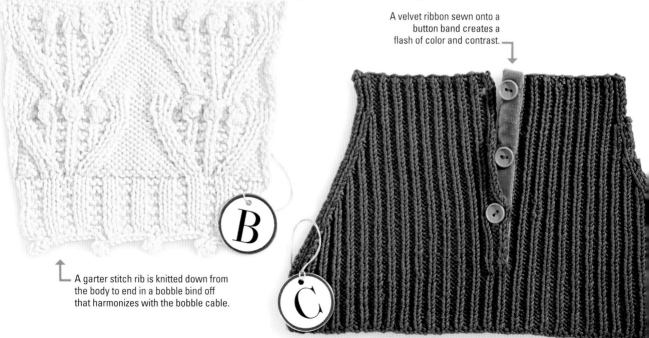

A garter stitch rib is knitted down from the body to end in a bobble bind off that harmonizes with the bobble cable.

B

A velvet ribbon sewn onto a button band creates a flash of color and contrast.

C

designing with details

sleeve, where some stitches are bound off on the body, perhaps with a few rows of decreasing afterward—the top of the sleeve is slotted into these bound-off stitches. This style has the advantage of not cutting too far into the body, and the stitch pattern is unaffected. A raglan armhole can be a very effective way to introduce detail into a very plain design; decorative borders can be worked next to the shaping. In **swatch A** I have used a cable between the outer edge and the fully fashioned shaping. A knit stitch at each end gives a neat edge, making it a perfect border for the armholes of a sleeveless summer top, and the cable carries up into the neckband.

Choosing the appropriate edging detail can be really rewarding. There are so many great edgings to choose from that selecting the right one becomes an art in itself. A delicate eyelet edging on a lacy design can look too fussy, so it isn't just about marrying up similar types of pattern—the balance has to be right.
In **swatch B**, my main pattern is a cable with bobbles, but I wanted a fairly simple edging that had a feature connected in some way to the cable. A garter stitch rib picked up and knitted down from the body to end in a bobble bind-off did the job. This edging is decorative, relates to the main pattern and doesn't compete with the body of the sweater. A simple ribbed collar can be finished with a picot bind-off to feminize it and make it prettier.

Buttons provide a great way to enhance a design. They can make a simple knit look more glamorous; big buttons can become a main feature. On **sample C**, I sewed a velvet ribbon on a button band. I like the way the flash of color just peeps through and the buttons contrast against the background. Another way to introduce elements into a knit is to add embellishment. This can be done through appliqué, embroidery or beading. I prefer to keep added-on interest fairly modest, because I don't want to detract from the knitted fabric and because you can go too far if you're not careful. A small piece of embroidery on a collar or pocket is best—plus you can run into wash and care problems if there is too much detail. Simple embroidery can look much more charming and folkloric and less like the mass-produced embroidered knits. Beading and sequins can be added to collars, cuffs or front bands to achieve a vintage effect. A crisp cotton yarn is perfect for enhancing an intricate stitch detail, while, conversely, a bulkier yarn will tend to maximize the impact of a simple stitch.

It's important to remember that the yarn used in each garment has been chosen carefully for its qualities to make the most of the design. Even when using the simplest types of detailing, such as a seed-stitch collar and bands on a stockinette stitch cardigan, you'll need to use a yarn that emphasizes the subtle patterning in your design. ■

Interested in adding detail to your knits? Try these tips:

▶ Sew beads onto parts of a Fair Isle sweater, such as the points of a diamond or star, or inside a cable.

▶ Embroider onto a collar of an existing garment.

▶ Change the buttons on a jacket—be adventurous! Perhaps gilt or large vintage buttons could make a rustic, country style look more edgy.

▶ Take a plain cardigan in a fine yarn, lengthen the sleeve rib and add four buttons on the side to give a Victorian blouse style. Or work it in a thicker yarn and add a collar and epaulettes for a more military style.

patterns

The three designs featured here encapsulate my detail philosophy.

Button Detail Top

The ribbed top is simplicity itself—two strips of knitting are fastened together by different-colored buttons. The depth of the neck is determined by how high or low you button it up—high and demure for day, low and glamorous for evening. You could use vintage buttons for an evening top or wooden buttons for a casual summer one. It is knitted in my Baby Cashmerino mix, which gives it the elasticity needed to make the ribbed body.

Cable Band Cardigan

This cardigan is a more complex design. The main cables are edged and defined by smaller ones, and a contrasting cable snakes around the yoke horizontally. The body is shaped to give a flattering tailored effect, but the style is softened by the addition of a picot edging. To achieve the prettiest picot edge, the body and sleeves were knit from the top down and a picot cast-off was used. There are turning rows so that the neck fits neatly around the shoulders. The design is knit in my extra-fine merino Rialto, in a double knitting weight to keep it lightweight.

Cardigan with Ribbed Sleeves

The ribbed yoke top has bell sleeves that echo the slightly flared body, which is achieved by the drawing in of stockinette stitch running into the ribbed yoke. It uses my bamboo/wool Prima yarn, which has the drape that gives the garment its swing. The slightly scooped neck maintains the feminine feel of the sleeves. A ribbon can be threaded through under the yoke for an even more feminine look.

Button Detail Top

This clever little top consists simply of two ribbed strips and contrasting buttons.

TO FIT BUST
81, 86, 92, 97, 102 cm
32, 34, 36, 38, 40 in

FINISHED MEASUREMENTS BUST
92, 96, 100, 106, 110 cm
36, 37¾, 39½, 41¾, 43¼ in

LENGTH TO SHOULDER
49, 51, 53, 56, 60 cm
19¼, 20, 21, 22, 23½ in

MATERIALS
● 7 (8, 8, 9, 10) 50g balls of Debbie Bliss Baby Cashmerino in Indigo 207.
● Pair 3.25mm (US 3) knitting needles.
● 22 (24, 24, 26, 28) small buttons in assorted colors.

TENSION
■ 27 sts and 38 rows to 10cm/4in over patt using 3.25mm (US 3) needles.

ABBREVIATIONS
See page 123.

108

LEFT FRONT/BACK
With 3.25mm (US 3) needles, cast on 65 (68, 71, 74, 77) sts.
1st row (right side) P1, k1, [p1, k2] to last 3 sts, p1, k1, p1.
2nd row K1, p1, k1, p to last 3 sts, k1, p1, k1.
These 2 rows form the patt and are repeated 184 (192, 199, 211, 226) times more, then the 1st row again, so ending with a right side row. [371 (387, 401, 425, 455) rows worked in total]
Cast off knitwise.

RIGHT FRONT/BACK
With 3.25mm (US 3) needles, cast on 65 (68, 71, 74, 77) sts.
1st row (right side) P1, k1, [p1, k2] to last 3 sts, p1, k1, p1.
2nd row K1, p1, k1, p to last 3 sts, k1, p1, k1.
These 2 rows form the patt.
1st buttonhole row (right side) P1, k1, yrn, yo (to make 2 sts), k2tog, k1, [p1, k2] to last 3 sts; p1, k1, p1.
2nd buttonhole row K1, p1, k1, p to last 4 sts, k1, p2tog tbl, k1.
Rep 1st and 2nd rows 7 times more.
Rep the last 16 rows 10 (11, 11, 12, 13) times more.
Rep 1st and 2nd rows 15 (7, 14, 10, 9) times more.
1st buttonhole row (right side) P1, k1, yrn, yo, k2tog, k1, [p1, k2] to last 3 sts, p1, k1, p1.
2nd buttonhole row K1, p1, k1, p to last 4 sts, k1, p2tog tbl, k1.
Rep 1st and 2nd rows 7 times more.
Rep the last 16 rows 9 (10, 10, 11, 12) times more.
Work the 2 buttonhole rows once more.
Patt 1 row, so ending with a right side row.
Cast off knitwise.

TO MAKE UP
Sew buttons to left front/back to match buttonholes on right front/back, then button the two pieces together. To form the side seams, fold pieces in half along the shoulder line, matching cast on and cast off edges, then join the seams, leaving approximately 16cm/6¼ in open for armholes. As the seam is joined from the lower edge up to the armhole, you can adjust the armhole depth to suit. Unbutton the two pieces to form the neck. ✽

notes
✽ The right side of the top is worked from lower front up to the shoulder and down to the lower back, with an integral buttonhole band. The left side is worked in the same way, omitting the buttonholes.
✽ Join in new yarn 3 sts in from either edge.

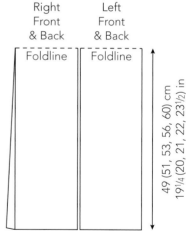

Right Front & Back   Left Front & Back

Foldline   Foldline

49 (51, 53, 56, 60) cm
19¼ (20, 21, 22, 23½) in

46 (48, 50, 53, 55) cm
18 (19, 19¾, 21, 21¾) in

Cable Band Cardigan

A cable top, knitted in different directions, with a semi-circular yoke—the intricate design is enhanced by delicate picot edgings.

TO FIT BUST
86, 92, 102 cm
34, 36, 38 in

FINISHED MEASUREMENTS
BUST
90, 95, 100 cm
35½, 37½, 39½ in

LENGTH
56cm/22in for all sizes

SLEEVE LENGTH
46cm/18in

MATERIALS
● 13 (13, 14) 50g balls of Debbie Bliss Rialto DK in Duck Egg 19.
● Pair each 3.25mm (US 3) and 4mm (US 6) knitting needles.
● 3.25mm (US 3) and 4mm (US 6) circular needles.
● Cable needle.
● 10 buttons.

TENSIONS
■ Panel A, 22 sts measure 6cm/2¼in, 32 rows to 10cm/4in; Panel B, 32 sts and 30 rows to 10cm/4in square and 22 sts and 30 rows to 10cm/4in square over st st, all using 4mm (US 6) needles.

PANEL A
Worked over 22 sts.
1st row (right side) P3, k3, C6F, p6, k3, p1.
2nd and every wrong side row K and p the sts as they appear.
3rd row P3, C6B, C5FP, p3, C4BP, p1.
5th row P2, C4BP, [C5FP] twice, C4BP, p2.
7th row P1, C4BP, p3, C5FP, C6B, p3.
9th row P1, k3, p6, C6F, k3, p3.
11th row P1, C4FP, p3, C5BP, C6B, p3.
13th row P2, C4FP, [C5BP] twice, C4FP, p2.
15th row P3, C6B, C5BP, p3, C4FP, p1.
16th row As 2nd row.
These 16 rows form Panel A patt.

PANEL B
Worked over 32 sts.
1st row (right side) [P2, k3] 6 times, p2.
2nd and every wrong side row K and p the sts as they appear.
3rd row P2, C3B, p2, k3, p2, C4FP, C4BP, p2, k3, p2, C3F, p2.
5th row P2, k3, p2, C4FP, p2, C6B, p2, C4BP, p2, k3, p2.
7th row P2, C3B, p3, [C4FP, C4BP] twice, p3, C3F, p2.
9th row P2, k3, p4, C6F, p2, C6F, p4, k3, p2.
11th row P2, C3B, p3, [C4BP, C4FP] twice, p3, C3F, p2.
13th row P2, k3, p2, C4BP, p2, C6B, p2, C4FP, p2, k3, p2.
15th row P2, C3B, p2, k3, p2, C4BP, C4FP, p2, k3, p2, C3F, p2.
16th row As 2nd row.
These 16 rows form the Panel B patt.

YOKE
Cable band With 4mm (US 6) needles, cast on 22 sts.
1st set-up row (right side) P3, k9, p6, k3, p1.
2nd set-up row K1, p3, k6, p9, k3.
Beg with the 1st row, work 290 rows in Panel A patt.
Work 1st set-up row again.
Cast off knitwise.
With right side of band facing, 3.25mm (US 3) circular needle

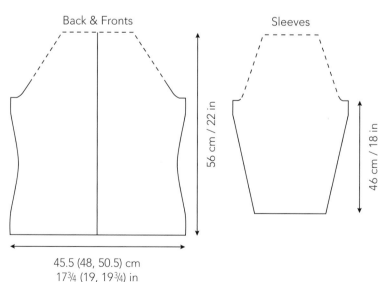

abbreviations

C3B = slip next 2 sts onto cable needle, hold at back of work, k1, then k2 from cable needle.

C3F = slip next st onto cable needle, hold at front of work, k2, then k1 from cable needle.

C4BP = slip next st onto cable needle, hold at back of work, k3, then p1 from cable needle.

C4FP = slip next 3 sts onto cable needle, hold at front of work, p1, then k3 from cable needle.

C5BP = slip next 2 sts onto cable needle, hold at back of work, k3, then p2 from cable needle.

C5FP = slip next 3 sts onto

cable needle, hold at front of work, p2, then k3 from cable needle.

C6B = slip next 3 sts onto cable needle, hold at back of work, k3, then k3 from cable needle.

C6F = slip next 3 sts onto cable needle, hold at front of work, k3, then k3 from cable needle.

kfb = knit into front and back of next st.

pfb = purl into front and back of next st.

yb = yarn to back of work.

yf = yarn to front of work.

yo = yarn over needle to make one st.

Also see page 123.

Back & Fronts

56 cm / 22 in

45.5 (48, 50.5) cm
17¾ (19, 19¾) in

Sleeves

46 cm / 18 in

Cable Band Cardigan

and joining yarn at end of last row (the lower pick up edge is on the left of the band, not at the edge where the first and last cables are) pick up and k294 sts from left side row-ends of cable band. With 4mm (US 6) needles, cast off loosely knitwise.
With 3.25mm (US 3) circular needle and inserting needle under 2 strands of each cast off st, pick up and k294 sts from cast off sts.

RIGHT FRONT
Set-up row (wrong side) With 4mm (US 6) needles work as follows: p8, [k2, p3] 6 times, k2, p6, pfb, p1, turn and complete right front on these 49 sts, leaving rem 246 sts on the circular needle for sleeves, back and left front.
Work in patt as follows:
1st row (right side) K9, work 32 sts of 1st row of Panel B, k8.
2nd row P8, work 32 sts of 2nd row of Panel B, p9.
These 2 rows set the position of Panel B with st st at each side. Working correct patt panel rows, cont in patt and work 16 more rows.
Shape armhole
Inc row (right side) K1, kfb, patt to end. 50 sts.
Cont in patt and inc in this way at beg of next 4 (6, 8) right side rows, taking inc sts into st st. 54 (56, 58) sts.
Patt 1 row.
Next row (right side) Cast on 4 (5, 6) sts (for underarm), patt to end. 58 (61, 64) sts.
Cont in patt, work 21 rows.
Shape side
Dec row (right side) K2, k2tog, patt to end. 57 (60, 63) sts.
Cont in patt, dec in this way at beg of 4 foll 8th rows.
53 (56, 59) sts.
Patt 11 rows.
Inc row (right side) K1, kfb, patt to end. 54 (57, 60) sts.
Cont in patt, inc in this way at beg of 2 foll 8th rows.
56 (59, 62) sts.
Patt 19 (15, 11) rows, so ending with 2nd row of 9th patt repeat.
Next row (right side) K16 (19, 22), [p2, k3] 6 times, p2, k8.
Change to 3.25mm (US 3) needles.
K 1 row.
Picot cast off row K2, cast off one st, [return st to left needle,

cast on 2 sts, cast off 4 sts] to end. Fasten off.

RIGHT SLEEVE
With wrong side facing and 4mm (US 6) needles, join yarn to 246 sts on circular needle at lower edge of cable band and work as follows:
Set-up row (wrong side) Pfb, p7, [k2, p3] 6 times, k2, p6, pfb, p1, turn and complete right sleeve on these 50 sts, leaving rem 198 sts on the circular needle for back, left sleeve and left front.
Work in patt as follows:
** **1st row** (right side) K9, work 32 sts of 1st row of Panel B, k9.
2nd row P9, work 32 sts of 2nd row of Panel B, p9.
These 2 rows set the position of Panel B with st st at each side. Working correct patt panel rows throughout, cont in patt and work 2 more rows.
Inc row (right side) K1, kfb, patt to last 3 sts, kfb, k2. 52 sts.
Cont in patt and inc in this way at each end of next 11 (13, 15) right side rows. 74 (78, 82) sts.
Patt 1 row.
Next row (right side) Cont in patt and cast on 4 (5, 6) sts at beg of next 2 rows for underarm. 82 (88, 94) sts.
Patt 10 rows.
Dec row (right side) K2, k2tog, patt to last 4 sts, skpo, k2. 80 (86, 92) sts.
Cont in patt and dec in this way at each end of 11 foll 8th rows. 58 (64, 70) sts.
Patt 33(29, 25) rows, so ending with 2nd row of 11th patt repeat.
Next row (right side) K13 (16, 19), [p2, k3] 6 times, p2, k13 (16, 19).
Change to 3.25mm (US 3) needles.
K 1 row.
Work picot cast off row as given for Right Front.
Fasten off.

BACK
With wrong side facing and 4mm (US 6) needles, join yarn to 198 sts on circular needle at lower edge of cable band and work as follows:
Set-up row (wrong side) Pfb, p7, [k2, p3] 6 times, k2, p22, [k2, p3]

Cable Band Cardigan

6 times, k2, p6, pfb, p1, turn and complete the back on these 104 sts, leaving rem 96 sts on the circular needle for left sleeve and left front.

Work in patt.

1st row (right side) K9, work 32 sts of 1st row of Panel B, k22, work 32 sts of 1st row of Panel B, k9.

2nd row P9, work 32 sts of 2nd row of Panel B, p22, work 32 sts of 2nd row of Panel B, p9.

These 2 rows set the position of two Panel B patts with st st between and at each side.

Working correct patt panel rows, cont in patt and work 16 more rows.

Shape armholes

Inc row (right side) K1, kfb, patt to last 3 sts, kfb, k2. 106 sts.

Cont in patt and inc in this way at each end of next 4(6, 8) right side rows, taking inc sts into st st. 114 (118, 122) sts.

Patt 1 row.

Cont in patt and cast on 4 (5, 6) sts (for underarm) at beg of next 2 rows. 122 (128, 134) sts.

Cont in patt for 20 rows.

Shape sides

Dec row (right side) K2, k2tog, patt to last 4 sts, skpo, k2. 120 (126, 132) sts.

Cont in patt, dec in this way at each end of 4 foll 8th rows. 112 (118, 124) sts.

Patt 11 rows.

Inc row (right side) K1, kfb, patt to last 3 sts, kfb, k2. 114 (120, 126) sts.

Cont in patt, inc in this way at each end of 2 foll 8th rows. 118 (124, 130) sts.

Patt 19 (15, 11) rows, so ending with 2nd row of 9th patt repeat.

Next row (right side) K16 (19, 22), [p2, k3] 6 times, p2, k22, [p2, k3] 6 times, p2, k16 (19, 22).

Change to 3.25mm (US 3) needles.

K 1 row.

Work picot cast off row in same way as Left Front.

Fasten off.

LEFT SLEEVE

With wrong side facing and 4mm (US 6) needles, join yarn to 96 sts on circular needle at lower edge of cable band and work as follows:

Set up row (wrong side) Pfb, p7, [k2, p3] 6 times, k2, p6, pfb, p1, turn and complete left sleeve on these 50 sts, leaving 48 sts on a holder for left front.

Work as given for Right Sleeve from ** to end.

LEFT FRONT

With 4mm (US 6) needles, join yarn to rem 48 sts on holder and work as follows:

Set up row (wrong side) Pfb, p7, [k2, p3] 6 times, k2, p8. 49 sts.

Work in patt as follows:

1st row (right side) K8, work 32 sts of 1st row of Panel B, k9.

2nd row P9, work 32 sts of 2nd row of Panel B, p8.

These 2 rows set the position of Panel B patt with st st at each side.

Working correct patt panel rows, cont in patt and work 16 more rows.

Shape armhole

Inc row (right side) Patt to last 3 sts, kfb, k2. 50 sts.

Cont in patt, inc in this way at end of next 4 (6, 8) right side rows. 54 (56, 58) sts.

Patt 2 rows.

Next row (wrong side) Cast on 4 (5, 6) sts (for underarm), patt to end. 58 (61, 64) sts.

Cont in patt for 20 rows.

Shape side

Dec row (right side) Patt to last 4 sts, skpo, k2. 57 (60, 63) sts.

Cont in patt and dec in this way at end of 4 foll 8th rows. 53 (56, 59) sts.

Patt 11 rows.

Inc row (right side) Patt to last 3 sts, kfb, k2. 54 (57, 60) sts.

Cont in patt, inc in this way at end of 2 foll 8th rows. 56 (59, 62) sts.

Patt 19 (15, 11) rows, so ending with 2nd row of 9th patt repeat.

Next row (right side) K8, [p2, k3] 6 times, p2, k16 (19, 22).

Change to 3.25mm (US 3) needles.

Cable Band Cardigan

K 1 row.
Work picot cast off row in same way as Right Front.
Fasten off.

YOKE

With right side facing and 3.25mm (US 3) circular needle, pick up and k148 sts along top edge of cable band.
With 4mm (US 6) needles, cast off loosely knitwise.
With 3.25mm (US 3) circular needle and inserting needle under 2 strands of each cast off st, pick up and k148 sts from cast off sts.
1st row (wrong side) K3, [p3, k2, p12, k2, p3, k2] 6 times, k1.
2nd row P3, [C3B, p2, k12, p2, C3F, p2] 6 times, p1.
3rd row As 1st row.
4th row P3, [k3, p2, k12, p2, k3, p2] 6 times, p1.
5th row As 1st row.
6th row P3, [C3B, p2, k1, k2tog, k6, skpo, k1, p2, C3F, p2] 6 times, p1. 136 sts.
7th row K3, [p3, k2, p10, k2, p3, k2] 6 times, k1.
8th row P3, [k3, p2, k10, p2, k3, p2] 6 times, p1.
9th row As 7th row.
10th row P3, [C3B, p2, k1, k2tog, k4, skpo, k1, p2, C3F, p2] 6 times, p1. 124 sts.
11th row K3, [p3, k2, p8, k2, p3, k2] 6 times, k1.
12th row P3, [k3, p2, k8, p2, k3, p2] 6 times, p1.
13th row As 11th row.
14th row P3, [C3B, p2, k1, k2tog, k2, skpo, k1, p2, C3F, p2] 6 times, p1. 112 sts.
15th row Yo, k3, [p3, k2, p6, k2, p3, k2] 6 times, kfb. 114 sts.
16th row K2, p2, [k1, k2tog, p2, k6, p2, skpo, k1, p2] 6 times, k2. 102 sts.
Do not break yarn, leave sts on needle and work collar.

COLLAR

1st row (right side of collar, wrong side of work) K4, [p2, k2] to last 2 sts, k2. 102 sts.
2nd row K2, [p2, k2] to end.
These 2 rows form rib with k2 garter st borders at each end.
Work 1 more row.

Shape back neck

1st row (wrong side of collar) Rib 88, yf, sl1, yb, turn.
2nd row Sl1, rib 74, sl1, yb, turn.
3rd row Sl1, yb, rib 66, yf, sl1, yb, turn.
4th row Sl1, rib 58, sl1, yb, turn.
5th row Sl1, yb, rib 50, yf, sl1, yb, turn.
6th row Sl1, rib 42, sl1, yb, turn.
7th row Sl1, yb, rib 34, yf, sl1, yb, turn.
8th row Sl1, rib 26, sl1, yb, turn.
9th row Sl1, yb, rib to last 2 sts, k2.
Cont in rib with k2 borders and work a further 27 rows across all 102 sts.
K 1 row.
Work picot cast off as given for Right Front.

BUTTON BAND

With right side facing and 3.25mm (US 3) needles, beg at start of collar on left front, pick up and k10 sts from row ends of yoke, 15 sts from cast off edge of cable band and 90 sts down left front edge. 115 sts.
K 8 rows.
Cast off loosely knitwise.

BUTTONHOLE BAND

With right side facing and 3.25mm (US 3) needles, beg at lower edge of right front, pick up and k90 sts up right front edge, 15 sts from cast on edge of cable band and 10 sts from row ends of yoke, ending at start of collar. 115 sts.
K 3 rows.
Buttonhole row (right side) K19, [skpo, yo, k2tog, k6] 9 times, skpo, yo, k2tog, k2.
Next row K, working twice into each yo.
K 3 more rows.
Cast off loosely knitwise.

TO MAKE UP

Join underarm seams. Join sleeves to back and fronts at armhole edges. Join side and sleeve seams. Sew on buttons. ❖

Cardigan with Ribbed Sleeves

A pretty summer top with a ribbed yoke echoed in the bell-shaped sleeves.

TO FIT BUST
81, 86, 92, 97 cm
32, 34, 36, 38 in

FINISHED MEASUREMENTS
(see NOTE)

BUST
81, 86, 92, 97 cm
32, 34, 36, 38 in

LENGTH
59, 60, 61, 62 cm
23¼, 23½, 2, 24½ in

SLEEVE
29 cm/11½ in for all sizes.

MATERIALS
● 12 (13, 15, 16) 50g balls
of Debbie Bliss Prima in
Leaf Green 12.
● Pair each 3.25mm (US 3),
3.75mm (US 5) and 4mm
(US 6) knitting needles.
● 4 buttons.

TENSION
■ 22 sts and 30 rows to
10cm/4in square over st st
using 4mm (US 6) needles.
28 sts and 32 rows to
10cm/4in square over twisted
rib using 3.75mm
(US 5) needles.

ABBREVIATIONS
See page 123.

BACK
With 4mm (US 6) needles, cast on 135 (143, 151, 159) sts.
1st row (right side) P1, [k1 tbl, p1] to end.
2nd row K1, [p1 tbl, k1] to end.
These 2 rows form twisted rib.
Rep the last 2 rows 4 times more.
Beg with a k row, work 4 rows in st st.
Dec row (right side) K6, skpo, k to last 8 sts, k2tog, k6.
Work 9 rows in st st.
Rep the last 10 rows 8 times more and the dec row again. 115 (123, 131, 139) sts.
Next row P to end.
Change to 3.75mm (US 5) needles.
Now work in twisted rib until back measures 40 (41, 41, 42)cm/15¾ (16, 16, 16½)in from cast on edge, ending with a wrong side row.

Shape armholes
Cast off 6 (6, 6, 8) sts at beg of next 2 rows. 103 (111, 119, 123) sts.
Dec row (right side) Rib 3, ssk, rib to last 5 sts, k2tog, rib 3.
Cont to dec in this way on next 5 (7, 9, 9) right side rows. 91 (95, 99, 103) sts.
Rib 35 (35, 35, 39) rows.

Shape neck
Next row (right side) Rib 29 (31, 33, 33) sts, turn and cont on these sts only for first side, leave rem sts on a spare needle.
Next row Rib 3, p2tog, rib to end.
Next row Rib to last 5 sts, k2tog, rib 3.
Rep the last 2 rows twice more. 23 (25, 27, 27) sts.
Rib 1 row.
Leave sts on a spare needle.
With right side facing, slip center 33 (33, 33, 37) sts onto a holder, rejoin yarn to rem 29 (31, 33, 33) sts, rib to end.
Next row (wrong side) Rib to last 5 sts, p2tog tbl, rib 3.
Next row Rib 3, ssk, rib to end.
Rep last 2 rows twice more. 23 (25, 27, 27) sts.
Rib 1 row.
Leave sts on a spare needle.

Cardigan with Ribbed Sleeves

LEFT FRONT

With 4mm (US 6) needles, cast on 71 (75, 79, 83) sts.

1st row (right side) P1, [k1 tbl, p1] to last 2 sts, k1 tbl, k1.

2nd row K1, [p1 tbl, k1] to end.

These 2 rows form twisted rib, with one k st at front edge on every row.

Rep the last 2 rows 4 times more.

Next row K to last 7 sts, p1, [k1 tbl, p1] twice, k1 tbl, k1.

Next row K1, [p1 tbl, k1] 3 times, p to end.

These 2 rows form st st with ribbed and garter st front edge. Work a further 2 rows.

Dec row (right side) K6, skpo, k to last 7 sts, p1, [k1 tbl, p1] 3 times.

Work 9 rows.

Rep the last 10 rows 8 times more and the dec row again. 61 (65, 69, 73) sts.

Next row P to end.

Change to 3.75mm (US 5) needles.

Now work in twisted rib with one k st at front edge on every row until front measures 40 (41, 41, 42)cm/15¾(16, 16, 16½)in from cast on edge, ending with a wrong side row.

Shape armhole

Cast off 6 (6, 6, 8) sts at beg of next row. 55 (59, 63, 65) sts.

Rib 1 row.

Dec row Rib 3, ssk, rib to end.

Cont to dec in this way on next 5 (7, 9, 9) right side rows. 49 (51, 53, 55) sts.

Rib 11 rows straight.

Shape neck

Next row (right side) Rib 35 (37, 39, 39) sts, turn and leave rem 14 (14, 14, 16) sts on a holder.

Rib 1 row.

Next row Rib to last 5 sts, k2tog, rib 3.

Next row Rib 3, p2tog, rib to end.

Rep the last 2 rows 5 times more. 23 (25, 27, 27) sts.

Rib 18 (18, 18, 22) rows straight.

Leave sts on a spare needle.

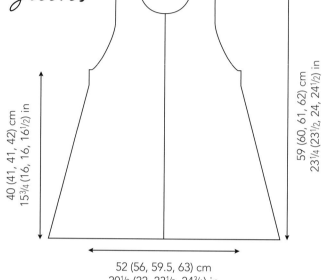

Back & Fronts

40 (41, 41, 42) cm
15¾ (16, 16, 16½) in

59 (60, 61, 62) cm
23¼ (23½, 24, 24½) in

52 (56, 59.5, 63) cm
20½ (22, 23½, 24¾) in

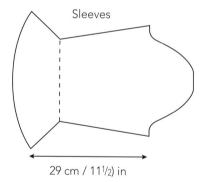

Sleeves

29 cm / 11½ in

RIGHT FRONT

Mark position for 4 buttons, the first on the first row of yoke, the 4th 3 rows below neck shaping and two spaced evenly between.

With 4mm (US 6) needles, cast on 71 (75, 79, 83) sts.

1st row (right side) K1, [k1 tbl, p1] to end.

2nd row K1, [p1 tbl, k1] to end.

These 2 rows form twisted rib with one k st at front edge on every row.

Rep the last 2 rows 4 times more.

Next row K1, [k1 tbl, p1] 3 times, k to end.

Cardigan with Ribbed Sleeves

Next row P to last 7 sts, k1, [p1 tbl, k1].
These 2 rows form st st with ribbed and garter st front edge. Work a further 2 rows.
Dec row (right side) K1, [k1 tbl, p1] 3 times, k to last 8 sts, k2tog, k6. Work 9 rows.
Rep the last 10 rows 8 times more and the dec row again. 61 (65, 69, 73) sts.
Next row P to end.
Change to 3.75mm (US 5) needles and work in twisted rib with one k st at front edge on every row.
Buttonhole row (right side) K1, k1 tbl, yo, k2tog, rib to end.
Work rem buttonholes to match markers.
Cont in twisted rib with garter st until front measures 40 (41, 41, 42)cm/15¾ (16, 16, 16½)in from cast on edge, ending with a right side row.

Shape armhole
Cast off 6 (6, 6, 8) sts at beg of next row. 55 (59, 63, 65) sts.
Dec row (right side) Rib to last 5 sts, k2tog, rib 3.
Cont to dec in this way on 5 (7, 9, 9) foll right side rows. 49 (51, 53, 55) sts.
Rib 9 rows straight, ending with a wrong side row.
Buttonhole row (right side) K1, k1 tbl, yo, k2tog, rib to end.
Rib 1 row.

Shape neck
Next row (right side) K14 (14, 14, 16) sts, leave these sts on a holder, patt to end. 35 (37, 39, 39) sts.
Next row Rib to end.
Next row Rib 3, ssk, rib to end.
Next row Rib to last 5 sts, p2tog tbl, rib 3.
Rep the last 2 rows 5 times more. 23 (25, 27, 27) sts.
Rib 18 (18, 18, 22) rows straight.
Leave sts on a spare needle.

SLEEVES
With 3.25mm (US 3) needles, cast on 125 (133, 141, 149) sts.
K 2 rows.
Change to 3.75mm (US 5) needles and work in twisted rib as given for Back and rib 38 rows.
Next row (right side) P1, [yarn to back, sl 1 purlwise, k2tog, psso, p1] to end. 63 (67, 71, 75) sts.
Rib 3 (3, 5, 5) rows straight.
1st inc row (right side) Rib 4, m1, rib to last 4 sts, m1, rib 4.
Cont to inc in this way on 5 foll 8th (8th, 6th, 6th) rows, then on 2 (2, 4, 6) foll 8th (8th, 6th, 4th) rows, taking inc sts into rib. 79 (83, 91, 99) sts.
Rib 3 rows straight, so ending with a wrong side row.

Shape top
Cast off 6 (6, 6, 8) sts at beg of next 2 rows. 67 (71, 79, 83) sts.
1st dec row (right side) Rib 3, ssk, rib to last 5 sts, k2tog, rib 3.
Cont to dec in this way on next 11 (12, 13, 14) right side rows. 43 (45, 51, 53) sts.
Next row (wrong side) Rib 3, p2tog, rib to last 5 sts, p2tog tbl, rib 3.
Next row (right side) Rib 3, ssk, rib to last 5 sts, k2tog, rib 3.
Rep the last 2 rows once more, then the first of these 2 rows again. 33 (35, 41, 43) sts.
Slipping first st of each group of cast off sts, cast off 3 sts in rib at beg of next 4 rows.
Cast off rem 21 (23, 29, 31) sts.

NECKBAND
Join left shoulder seam as follows: put each group of left shoulder sts onto a needle, with right sides tog and using 3.75mm (US 5) needle, cast off both sets of sts together knitwise, taking one st from each needle tog each time. Join right shoulder to match.
With right side facing and 3.25mm (US 3) circular needle, slip 14 (14, 14, 16) sts from right front neck onto needle, pick up and k16 (20, 16, 20) sts to shoulder, 8 sts down right back neck, k33 (33, 33, 37) sts from back neck, pick up and k 8 sts up left back neck and 16 (20, 16, 20) sts down left front neck, then k across 14 (14, 14, 16) sts at left front. 109 (117, 109, 125) sts.
Cast off knitwise.

TO MAKE UP
Extend cast on edge of sleeve peplums as far as they will go (it will form a semi-circle) and press. Press remaining parts lightly. Sew sleeves into armholes, easing to fit. Join side and sleeve seams. Sew on buttons. ❖

Abbreviations

alt alternate

beg beginning

cont continue

dec decrease

foll following

inc increase

k knit

kfb knit into front and back of stitch

m1 make one stitch by picking up the loop lying between the stitch just worked and next stitch and working into back of it

p purl

pfb purl into front and back of stitch

patt pattern

psso pass slipped stitch over

rem remaining

rep repeat

skpo slip 1, knit 1, pass slipped stitch over

sk2togpo slip one, knit 2 together, pass slipped stitch over

s2togkpo slip 2 stitches together, knit 1, pass 2 slipped stitches over

sl slip

ssk [sl 1 knitwise] twice, insert tip of left needle from left to right through front of both stitches and k2tog

st(s) stitch(es)

st st stocking stitch

tbl through back loop

tog together

yb yarn to back of work

yf yarn to front of work

yo yarn over needle to make one st

yrn yarn around needle

Glossary

bind off: To finish off an edge and keep stitches from unraveling by lifting the first stitch over the second, the second over the third, etc. (U.K.: cast off)

bind off in ribbing: Maintain the rib pattern as you bind off (knit the knit stitches; purl the purl stitches). (U.K.: cast off in ribbing)

cast on: Form a foundation row by making specified number of loops on the knitting needle.

decrease: Reduce the number of stitches in a row (e.g., knit 2 together; purl 2 together).

increase: Add to the number of stitches in a row (e.g., knit in front and back of stitch).

knitwise: Insert the needle into the stitch as if you were going to knit it.

make one: With tip of needle, lift strand between last stitch knit and next stitch on left-hand needle, place strand on left-hand needle and knit into back of it to increase one stitch.

place markers: Loop a piece of contrasting yarn or a purchased stitch marker onto the needle.

pick up and knit (purl): Knit (or purl) into the loops along an edge.

purlwise: Insert the needle into stitch as if you were going to purl it.

selvedge stitch: Edge stitch that helps make seaming easier.

skip: Skip specified number of stitches of the previous row and work into next stitch. (U.K.: miss)

slip, slip, knit (purl): Slip next two sts knitwise (purlwise), one at a time, to right-hand needle. Insert tip of left-hand needle into fronts of these sts from left to right and knit (purl) them together to decrease one st.

slip stitch: In knitting, pass a stitch from the left-hand to the right-hand needle as if to purl without working it. In crochet, insert hook through loop or edge, yarn over and pull through loop on hook. (U.K.: abbreviation—ss or sc)

work even: Continue in specified pattern without increasing or decreasing. (U.K.: work straight)

yarn over: In knitting, make a new stitch by placing the yarn over the right-hand needle. (U.K.: yfwd, yon, yrn) In crochet, wind yarn around hook. (U.K.: yoh or yrh)

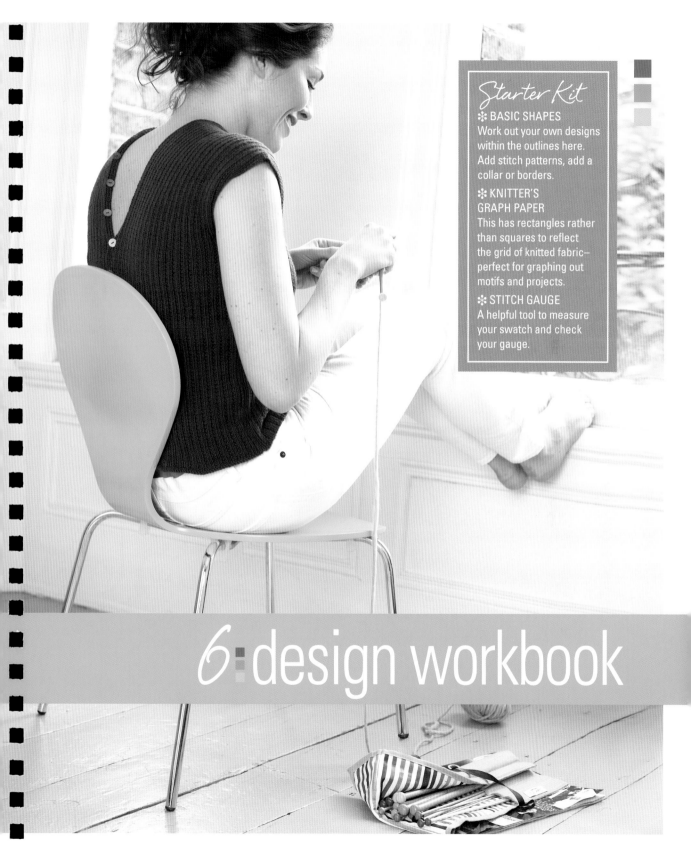

6: design workbook

Simple Shell

A simple shell provides a blank canvas. Leave with no edgings
or add borders and a stitch pattern.

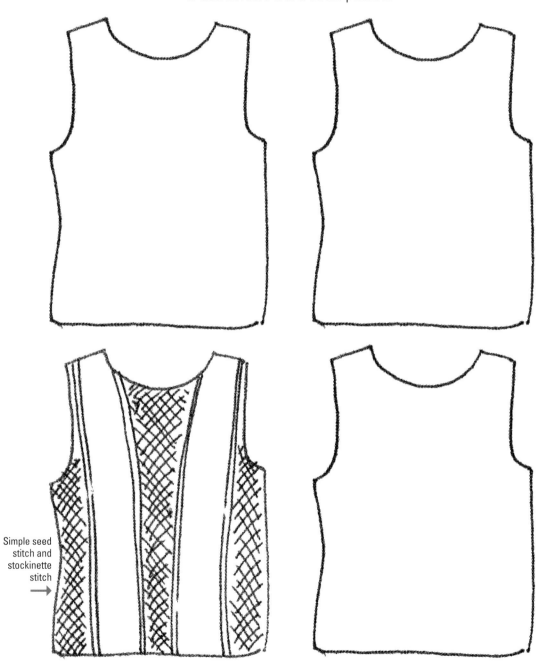

Simple seed stitch and stockinette stitch

Short-Sleeved Sweater

A short-sleeved top can have different patterns on the body and sleeves or if knitted in a rib fabric will shape in. Divide the front in two and make a cardigan.

The neckline could have a deeper scoop

A simple narrow rib becomes a wider flat rib to add extra stitch interest

Divide front and make into a cardigan

Generous Sweater

A dropped shoulder allows for heavier patterning to be taken to the full width as there are no armholes. The sleeves are shorter than normal as the shoulder "drops" over the top of the arm.

← Neat shawl collar added

All-over cable pattern

Pattern runs down into rib

Shaped Sides Sweater

With shaped sides you will need a simple selvedge stitch with a small repeat such as a seed stitch to shape in. Big pattern details are best kept central.

Add a turtleneck collar with cable continuing

Seed stitch background

Large central cable

132

A-Line Jacket

This shape can be achieved by shaping at the sides or decreasing within the body. This is one of the most flattering shapes.

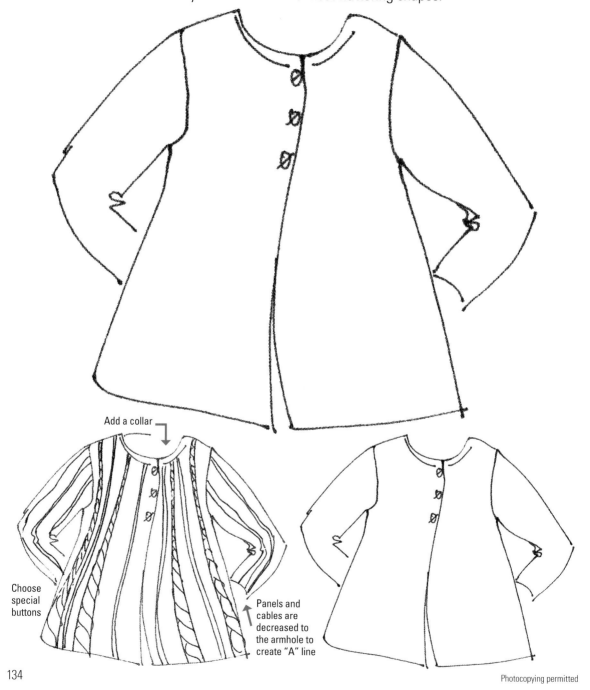

Add a collar

Choose special buttons

Panels and cables are decreased to the armhole to create "A" line

Fitted Jacket

Fitted jackets work best in simple stitches, and a neat armhole is best for a tailored effect. In a reversible fabric the collar can be worked into the fronts to avoid an ugly pick-up seam.

A rib brings in the waist

Cable is wider at lower hem to create slight flare

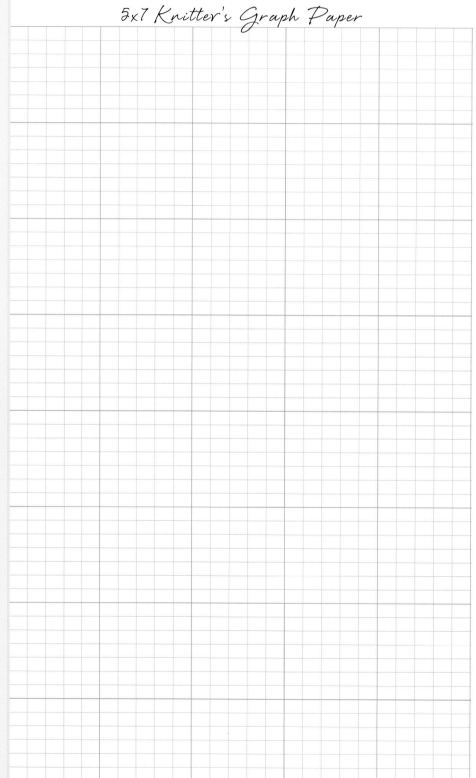

Notes

138

5x7 Knitter's Graph Paper

Notes

6x8 Knitter's Graph Paper

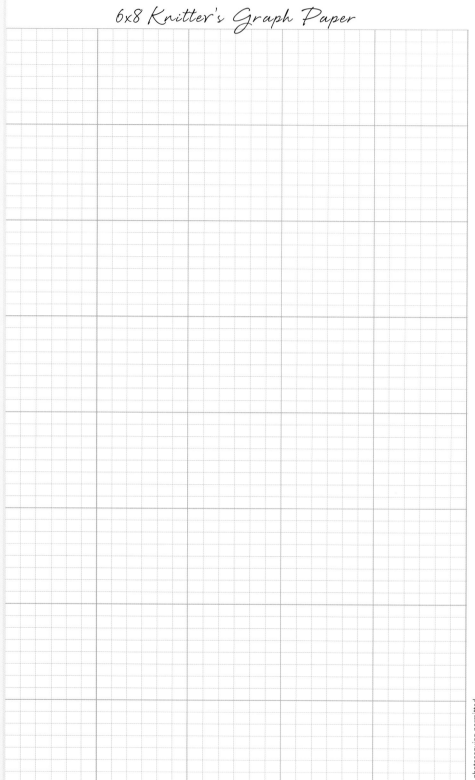

6x8 Knitter's Graph Paper

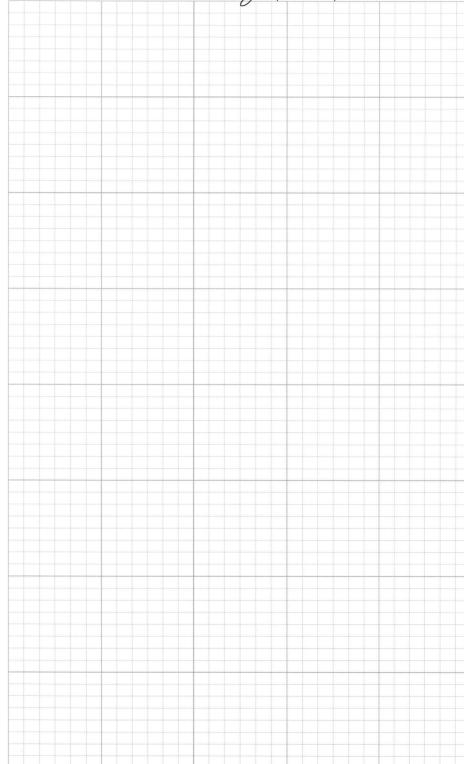

About the Yarns

The yarns I chose to use in this book are classic and enduring. When I first launched my range of yarns, I chose fibers and constructions that reflected the way I design. Although the fashion was for fancy yarns, I knew that my style was to design in texture and color, and so I needed smooth yarns that showed off the stitches.

All the designs were created with a specific yarn in mind for drape, stitch detail and softness. It's important wherever possible to use the yarn quoted in the pattern, or a comparable substitute, to avoid disappointment. Using a synthetic yarn instead of a natural one can produce a floppy fabric; inferior yarn may lack clarity of stitch. Substituting cotton for a wool or wool mix in a cabled pattern will eliminate elasticity, resulting in a wider garment. This is a guide to the yarns I have used in this publication.

DEBBIE BLISS BABY CASHMERINO
A lightweight yarn between a four-ply and double knitting weight.
Merino wool, microfiber, cashmere mix
Approx 125m/50g ball

DEBBIE BLISS CASHMERINO DOUBLE KNITTING
Merino wool, microfiber, cashmere mix
Approx 110m/50g ball

DEBBIE BLISS CASHMERINO ARAN
Merino wool, microfiber, cashmere mix
Approx 90m/50g ball

DEBBIE BLISS RIALTO DOUBLE KNITTING
Extrafine merino wool
Approx 105m/50g ball

DEBBIE BLISS RIALTO ARAN
Extrafine merino wool
Approx 80m/50g ball

DEBBIE BLISS LUXURY TWEED
Wool, angora mix
Approx 88m/50g ball

Blocking and pressing

"Blocking" means pinning out the pieces of your garment to see if their measurements are correct before sewing the seams. It is not always necessary, but it is very useful if you need to press the pieces because of uneven fabric or to adjust the size of them.

1 With the pieces wrong side up on a flat, padded surface, pin them at 1" intervals through the edge of the knitting into the padded surface. Check that the measurements are correct and that the stitches and rows are straight horizontally and vertically.

2 Check the ball band to see if there is any information on pressing. If there isn't, as a general rule, wool, linen, cotton and other natural yarns can be steamed thoroughly with no problem. Do not iron 100-percent synthetics; if the yarn is a synthetic/natural fiber mixture, use a cool iron over a dry cloth.

3 Cover the areas with a damp or dry cloth depending on the yarn. Press lightly and evenly, making sure you do not drag the fabric underneath, and avoid ribbed pieces.

4 Leave the pieces to dry completely before removing them from the cloth.

5 Sew seams.

Caring for your knitted garments

❊ Except for the Luxury Tweed, all of the yarns used in this book are machine washable.

❊ Read the symbols on the ball band and program your washing machine accordingly. Most hand knits are washed on gentle cycle in cool water.

❊ Some knitters still prefer to hand-wash their knits so that they last longer over time. Use lukewarm water and a soap, preferably liquid. Gently squeeze out excess moisture before you lift the garment out of the water so that the weight of the water doesn't stretch the garment.

❊ Whether machine- or hand-washed, lay the garment flat on an absorbent cloth, such as a towel. I like to measure the knit to make sure that it hasn't stretched and then reshape it to the original measurements.

Buying Yarns

❊ Check the ball band when buying your yarn—it will have all the information you need about tension, yardage, weight and needle size. Yarns are dyed in batches, and a single color can vary considerably, so you need to buy all the yarn you need for the project from the same dye lot. If the store does not have all you need of one dye lot, use the different ones on the neckband or borders, where the shade change won't show as much. If you know that you sometimes need more than the pattern states, buy an extra ball. All yarn amounts in the patterns are approximate; they are based on how much the knitter who made the sample garment used to complete a particular size, and your tension may require a different quantity. It's not uncommon to end up with an extra ball at the end.

Little Buddy Jacket

from page 98

KNITTED MEASUREMENTS
WIDTH (circumference): 4½"/11.5 cm
LENGTH (collar to waist): 1½"/4cm
MATERIALS One pair size 2 (2.75mm) knitting needles ● Scrap yarn for holding sts ● Tapestry needle ● C/2 Crochet hook
GAUGE 24 sts and 32 rows = 4"/10cm over garter st using size 2 (2.75) needles.

BACK AND FRONT
With size 2 (2.75mm) needles and CC, cast on 28 sts. Change to MC and work in garter st for ¾"/2cm. **Next RS row** K6, bind off 1 st, slip last 6 sts worked to scrap yarn (for left front), k to last 6 sts, sl next 6 sts (for right front) to scrap yarn, turn, bind off 1 st and cont on 14 back sts until piece measures 1½"/4cm. **Next RS row** Bind off using CC.
LEFT & RIGHT FRONTS
(work separately) Slip sts from scrap yarn to needle, cont in garter st until front matches back, bind off in cc.

SLEEVES
With CC, cast on 14 sts. Change to MC. Work in garter st until sleeve measures ¾"/2cm. Bind off.

FINISHING
Assemble pieces. With crochet hook and CC, slipstitch up the right front edge of jacket. With tapestry needle and CC, work 3 french knots along left front edge.❊

Worldwide Distributors

For stockists of Debbie Bliss yarns please contact:

AUSTRALIA/NEW ZEALAND
Prestige Yarns Pty Ltd
P O Box 39
Bulli NSW 2516
Australia
T: +61 02 4285 6669
info@prestigeyarns.com
www.prestigeyarns.com

BELGIUM/HOLLAND
Pavan
Thomas Van Theemsche
Meerlaanstraat 73
9860 Balegem (Oostrezele)
Belgium
T: +32 (0) 9 221 85 94
F: +32 (0) 9 221 56 62
pavan@pandora.be

BRAZIL
Quatro Estacoes Com
Las Linhas e Acessorios Ltda
Av. Das Nacoes Unidas
12551-9 Andar
Cep 04578-000 Sao Paulo
Brazil
T: +55 11 3443 7736
cristina@4estacoeslas.com/br

CANADA
Diamond Yarns Ltd
155 Martin Ross Avenue Unit 3
Toronto, Ontario M3J 2L9
T: +1 416 736 6111
F: +1 416 736 6112
www.diamondyarn.com

DENMARK
Fancy Knit
Hovedvejen 71
8586 Oerum Djurs
Ramten
T: +45 59 4621 89
roenneburg@mail.dk

FINLAND
Duo Design
Kaikukuja 1 c 31
00530 Helsinki
T +358 (0) 9 753 1716
maria.hellbom@priima.net
www.duodesign.fi

**GERMANY/AUSTRIA/
SWITZERLAND/LUXEMBOURG**
**Designer Yarns
(Deutschland) GmbH**
Sachsstrasse 30
D-50259 Pulheim-Brauweiler
Germany
T: +49 (0) 2234 205453
F: +49 (0) 2234 205456
info@designeryarns.de
www.designeryarns.de

ICELAND
Storkurinn ehf
Laugavegi 59
101 Reykjavík
Iceland
T: +354 551 8258
F: +354 562 8252
storkurinn@simnet.is

MEXICO
Estambres Crochet SA de CV
Aaron Saenz 1891-7
Col. Santa Maria
Monterrey
N.L. 64650
T: +52 81 8335 3870
abremer@redmundial.com.mx

SPAIN
Oyambre Needlework SL
Balmes, 200 At.4
08006 Barcelona
T: +34 (0) 93 487 26 72
F: +34 (0) 93 218 6694
info@oyambreonline.com

SWEDEN
Nysta garn och textil
Luntmakargatan 50
S-113 58 Stockholm
T: +46 (0) 8 612 0330
nina@nysta.se
www.nysta.se

U. K.
Designer Yarns Ltd
Units 8–10
Newbridge Industrial Estate
Pitt Street, Keighley
W. Yorkshire BD21 4PQ
United Kingdom
T: +44 (0)1535 664222
F: +44 (0)1535 664333
alex@designeryarns.uk.com
www.designeryarns.uk.com

U. S. A
Knitting Fever Inc.
315 Bayview Avenue
Amityville, NY 11701
T: +1 516 546 3600
F: +1 516 546 6871
www.knittingfever.com

For more information
on my other books
and yarns, please visit:
www.debbieblissonline.com

Acknowledgments

This book would not have been possible without the
collaboration of the following people:

Rosy Tucker and Melody Griffiths, who are such an integral
part of what I do and whose generous creative contibution on this
publication has been inspirational.

Richard Burns, the photographer, whose beautiful pictures captured the
mood so well and who is such a joy to work with, and his lovely assistant Zoe.

Mia Pejcinovic, the terrific stylist who gave the garments
and the book such a fresh look.

Sally Klavheim, the great hair and makeup artist.

Rosy Tucker for the tremendous skill she brings to the pattern checking.

Penny Hill, for the technical wizardry of pattern compiling.

Wendy Williams, a great and very patient editor.

Diane Lamphron for the terrific book design.

The brilliant models Alex, Emma, Elijah, Frankie and Isabelle.

Heather Jeeves, my wonderful agent.

 Trisha Malcolm whose tremendous support of my work over the
years has meant such a lot to me.

Art Joinnides for making it possible.

The lastly, the amazing knitters who work to impossible deadlines:
Brenda Bostock, Pat Church, Barbara Clapham, Shirley Kennett,
Maisie Lawrence and Frances Wallace.